Database Programming
with JDBC and Java

THE JAVA SERIES™

Database Programming
with JDBC and Java

George Reese

O'REILLY™

Cambridge · Köln · Paris · Sebastopol · Tokyo

Database Programming with JDBC and Java
by George Reese

Copyright © 1997 O'Reilly & Associates, Inc. All rights reserved.
Printed in the United States of America.

Published by O'Reilly & Associates, Inc., 101 Morris Street, Sebastopol, CA 95472.

Editor: Andy Oram

Production Editors: Nancy Wolfe Kotary and Kismet McDonough-Chan

Printing History:

June 1997:   First Edition.

This book is printed on acid-free paper with 85% recycled content, 15% post-consumer waste. O'Reilly & Associates is committed to using paper with the highest recycled content available consistent with high quality.

ISBN: 1-56592-270-0   [8/97]

For Baa and Nonie

Table of Contents

Preface

It is never too late to become reasonable and wise;
but if the insight comes late, there is always
more difficulty in starting the change.

—Immanuel Kant
Prolegomena to Any Future Metaphysics

I began writing this book in May 1996 as Java celebrated one of its first major rites of passage, the inaugural JavaOne conference. The conference's underlying theme was Java's transition from an applet language to a hard-core computing environment. In the year since that conference, that theme has been growing into a reality. This book captures a small piece of that reality: Java as a language for enterprise computing.

Enterprise computing, a vague term used mostly to sell business systems development products, traditionally refers to the mission-critical systems on which a business depends. It almost always includes a database. At the heart of Java's enterprise computing philosophy lie the distributed computing and database access APIs—RMI and JDBC, respectively. Older languages require third-party APIs to provide this kind of support. Java, on the other hand, includes these features into the central Java distribution you will find on every Java platform. As a developer, you can write distributed applications that run against relational databases and know that those applications will run on any system on which you deploy them.

What exactly are these APIs? JDBC—the basic component to this book—allows you to write applications that access relational databases without any thought as to which particular database you are using. If you have ever had experience programming to more than one database API, you will definitely appreciate this aspect of Java. When you write a Java database program, that same program will run against

Oracle, Sybase, Ingres, Informix, mSQL, Postgres, or any other database that supports this API.

RMI, on the other hand, gives real meaning to the expression "the network is the computer." If you have written Internet applications in the past, you have probably been faced with the challenge of writing TCP/IP or UDP/IP sockets. While socket programming in Java is not nearly as hard as it is in other programming languages, the task of writing sockets is generally a side technical issue that takes time away from the writing of your main application code. By using distributed object technology, you can build Java objects that run on different machines but communicate with one another through simple Java method calls.

How do these APIs make Java something more than a simple applet building language? Database access is the core requirement of the majority of mission-critical business applications that get developed. By giving Java database access combined with the development of GUI development tools, JavaSoft has made Java a language that competes with established tools such as VisualBasic and PowerBuilder. Java distributed object support goes a giant step beyond these tools by liberating Java components from the need to be located together in the same Java Virtual Machine.

Audience

If you have not yet read a book on Java, then this book should not be the first one you pick up. I assume that readers have a basic understanding of the Java programming language. Specifically, you should feel comfortable with the basic syntax of Java and central concepts such as classes, interfaces, and packages. If you are looking for a starter book for Java programming, I strongly recommend *Exploring Java* by Patrick Niemeyer and Joshua Peck (O'Reilly & Associates).

I also expect that you know some basic database concepts. You do not need the solid foundation here that I am assuming for Java. Specifically, you should understand what a relational database is; know what tables, columns, and rows are; and understand basic SQL syntax. I do provide a basic introduction to these concepts in Chapter 2; however, this introduction is very quick and certainly misses a lot of important details. While Chapter 2 does not provide nearly enough knowledge to make you a database expert, it will serve you well if you intend to study databases while using this book. If you are truly green to the database world and really want to dive in, I suggest downloading a copy of the mSQL database at *http://Hughes.com.au,* which will provide you with enough of a database tutorial to get you started on this book.

Using This Book

I have tried to break out the API chapters from the rest of the book so that they might provide a good reference long after you understand the subject matter of this book. To that end, Chapters 4, 5, and 8 are geared exclusively to providing detailed discussion of the JDBC and RMI. Chapter 3 introduces client/server design in the Java world and prepares you for the classes we will build in Chapters 6 and 7. Chapters 6 and 7 thus build on the design work of Chapter 3 to put to practical use the database access tools covered in Chapters 4 and 5.

How you make use of this structure depends largely on your background. If you have done a lot of object-oriented client/server development, the information in Chapter 3 may be familiar to you. In that case, skimming the first couple of chapters for new information and hitting Chapter 4 head on might be your best approach. For people who simply have some database knowledge and a solid Java background, it might be a good idea to take the book sequentially, one chapter at a time.

Throughout this book, I have made sure the examples use `javadoc` commenting. If you are not familiar with `javadoc`, it is a utility that ships with the Sun JDK. By using the `javadoc` format, you can automatically generate Web pages that document your Java classes. The persistence library that gets developed later in the book has Web documentation at *http://www.ora.com/catalog/java-data/persistence/*. While using `javadoc` comments takes more space, I believe that it is good programming practice and that it also increases the readability of the examples in this book.

Software and Versions

In developing the examples in this book, I used JDK 1.1b3, and JDK 1.1 Final. I performed database access for all of the book except Chapter 5 using the mSQL 1.0.16 database engine with the mSQL-JDBC 0.96 JDBC driver. I handled database access for Chapter 5 using PersonalOracle 7.2.2.3.1 with the WebLogic beta Oracle driver. I tested the application server developed in Chapter 6 on both Solaris 2.5.1 and Windows NT 4.0. The client was tested on Windows 95, Windows NT 4.0, and Solaris 2.5.1.

Conventions Used in This Book

Italic is used for:

• Pathnames, filenames, and program names

• Internet addresses, such as domain names and URLs

`Constant width` is used for:

- Anything that might appear in a Java program, including keywords, method names, variables names, class names, and interface names

- Command lines and options that should be typed verbatim on the screen

- Tags that might appear in an HTML document

Examples of the programs in this book may be retrieved online from *ftp.ora.com* in */pub/examples/java/jdbc*. The files are on the site as *examples.tar.gz*.

Request for Comments

We invite you to help us improve our books. If you have an idea that could make this book more useful, or if you find a bug in an example or an error in the text, let us know by sending mail to *bookquestions@oreilly.com*.

About the Philosophers

If you read prefaces, it is even possible that you read author biographies as well. Mine notes that I came out of college with a degree in philosophy. The path from philosophy to Java programming is of course not a very common one; I nevertheless honestly believe that philosophy provides a very solid grounding for programming logic and object-oriented systems development.

During the first JavaOne conference, I attended an address being given by Dr. John Gage of Sun. In that speech, he quoted a modern philosopher of language and metaphysics, Dr. Donald Davidson. If you do not have a background in philosophy, chances are that you do not recognize his name. I was so amazed at hearing his name mentioned, I went up and spoke to Dr. Gage after the address. We got into a discussion of philosophy and computing during which he suggested I work philosophy quotes into the book. I have taken his advice and started each chapter with a quote from a major philosopher.

I have tried to choose quotes that have direct relevance to the topic at hand. In some cases, however, the quotes are only indirectly relevant. Most of the philosophers except Chomsky, Dennet, Descartes, and Kant come from a short period of time between the 1890s and 1950s. Kant wrote in the late 1700s, Descartes in the 1600s, and Chomsky and Dennet still write today.

Acknowledgments

While my name is the one that appears on the cover, this book would not be the book it is without the help of Andy Oram, the editor. I cannot thank him enough for the difference he has made in each chapter of this book. His efforts have helped make the difference between this being any Java book and it being an O'Reilly Java book.

A host of other people have influenced me in ways that both directly and indirectly have affected the quality of this book. First, there are those who have provided me with direct feedback on portions of the book: Monique Girgis, Ryan Olson, and Paul Wouters. Another group provided me with detailed feedback on the entire book: Dave Andreasen, Leigh Caldwell, Jim Farley, Patrick Killelea, Howard Melman, and Tim O'Reilly. Then there are those whose mentoring has provided me with the systems development skills that are key to the type of programming in this book: Steven Craig, Scott Hayman, Mark Kale, Tim King, and Dan Reagan. Finally, Monique deserves a special thanks for suggesting that I write this book in the first place.

It takes a lot of people other than the author and editor to create a book. At O'Reilly, I would like to thank Tim O'Reilly for publishing what I believe are the best books in the business. Kismet McDonough-Chan and Nancy Wolfe Kotary shared the jobs of production editor and project manager. Edie Freedman designed the eye-catching front cover for this book; Nancy Priest created the interior design; and Chris Reilley created the technical illustrations. Nicole Gipson Arigo provided quality control assurance. Madeleine Newell provided production assistance. Seth Maislin wrote the index.

Oh, and as cheesy as it sounds, I can't forget to thank my cats, Misty and Gypsy, just for being there.

Feedback for the Author

I have done everything in my power both to explain the JDBC and RMI APIs as well as to provide a practical infrastructure in which you might use them. I hope this book serves you well as you tackle database programming in Java. In that spirit, I would like very much to hear your comments, corrections, praise, or criticism. You can contact me at *borg@imaginary.com.*

I

DISTRIBUTED JAVA DATABASE APPLICATION DEVELOPMENT

The first section of this book takes you through distributed Java database application design and development with a focus on two Java Enterprise APIs: JDBC and RMI.

In this chapter:
• *Is Java Ready for Prime Time?*
• *Adding the Power of a Database to Java*
• *What Java Adds to Database Programming*

1

Beyond the Applet

Behold, I am a herald of the lightning and a heavy drop from the cloud; but this lightning is called overman.

—Friedrich Nietzsche
Also Sprach Zarathustra

Nietzsche tells the story of Zarathustra, a prophet who declares the coming of the *overman*, humanity's reaching beyond itself to evolve into something more. Like Zarathustra loudly proclaiming a new humanity, introductory books on Java tell the tale of an amazing convergence of the Internet tidal wave and Sun's portable programming language that heralds the coming of a new programming era. Java attracted much of its early attention with a promise to spice up static Web HTML documents with embedded applications such as the now ubiquitous animation applets. Though other programming tools provided differing levels of dynamic content to Web pages before Java arrived, none enabled browsers to process information at the browser level without requiring the user to download and install proprietary plug-ins.

In spite of all of its exciting promises, the Java story still remains incomplete. In the process of giving Web developers a tool for making fancier Web pages, Java also gave programmers a single guaranteed execution environment for all potential applications. Acceptance as an all-around programming language for application development requires that Java deliver not only its exciting promises, but also the features we expect to find in any programming language. To this end, several new chapters have been added to the Java story. This book explains just one of these chapters—how Java interacts with databases.

To create an application that runs on every possible architecture, a Java developer needs to write the application only once and to compile it once. By freeing us from the constraints of programming to a specific platform, Java provides a power much greater than applet programming for Web pages. A business that uses different platforms in different departments, such as Macintoshes in marketing, Suns in Information Systems, and Intel everywhere else, can now use Java to write corporate applications that run everywhere after just one compile.

Even portability among Windows, Macintosh, and UNIX platforms undersells the potential that Java offers. Quite a bit of hype has centered around the Network Computer (NC), a machine that uses the Java Virtual Machine as its basic operating environment. The NC has little or no disk space, but instead loads applications from servers located out on the company's Intranet, or even out on the Internet. You might see the NC as a throwback to the days of the dumb terminal, and thus doubt the viability of the NC. The success or failure of today's NC, however, is actually immaterial to the underlying concept of the network as the computer. With executable content entirely portable, programs may run on any number of Java devices we do not currently view as computers. Your cellular phone with its Java chip may have a program to access phone numbers created by your Windows contact management database.

Is Java Ready for Prime Time?

All of Java's potential has little meaning if it cannot perform the common tasks we have come to rely on in other languages. I hear the question "Is Java ready for prime time?" from managers and developers several times a week. People are dazzled by the thought of never again worrying about portability issues, but they have a lot of time and money invested in tools like C, C++, Delphi, and Power-Builder. We all have seen the promises of new technology go the way of the hula hoop, and many people have been burned by those fads. It is therefore quite natural to wonder first if Java is simply a flash in the pan, and second if it has the power to build mission-critical enterprise applications.

Java has traveled well beyond the realms of most programming languages by expanding its language specification to include APIs for accessing all kinds of computing resources. In contrast, other languages rely on third-party software vendors who often provide a variety of incompatible APIs to perform tasks such as 2D animation. Java's multimedia API, however, defines a single solution for proper 2D animation as part of the Java platform specification.

The JDK 1.0 release implemented what JavaSoft termed the Java Core API—the basic objects required for a minimally viable language. The Java platform specification has since grown to encompass many other APIs. The following is a list of the Java APIs at the time of this book's publication:

JavaBeans

In response to the Microsoft ActiveX threat, JavaSoft has developed Java-Beans, a platform-neutral specification for creating software components. Part of the JavaBeans specification actually involves interfacing with ActiveX components.

Java Commerce

Java commerce is an Internet-based API for providing secure economic transactions across an insecure network. This API includes Java Wallet, which is a framework for client-side credit card, debit card, and electronic cash transactions.

Java Core

These are the libraries that shipped with the JDK 1.0 release. It consists of the `java.applet`, `java.awt`, `java.io`, `java.lang`, `java.net`, and `java.util` packages and provides the core level of functionality needed in order to build simple applets and applications in Java.

Java Embedded

The Java embedded API enables devices such as cellular phones and toasters, which may not be capable of supporting the full range of Java core functionality, to offer a subset of Java core.

Java Enterprise

Java enterprise actually consists of three separate libraries for providing access to an organization's resources and applications. The Java DataBase Connectivity API, or JDBC, provides database connectivity. Using JDBC, an application can perform database access independent of the actual database engine being used for data storage. The same application can be written once, compiled once, and run against any database engine with a JDBC driver. Chapters 4 and 5 provide a detailed discussion of the JDBC API.

The Interface Definition Language (IDL) enables Java applications to provide a language-neutral interface between Java objects and objects located across the network. It follows the Object Management Group (OMG) IDL specification.

Remote Method Invocation, or RMI, is a Java-specific API that lets objects call methods in objects located across the network. Unlike IDL, RMI is a Java-only solution. Instead of writing complex communication protocols using sockets, an application can communicate with remote objects through simple Java method calls. Chapter 8 discusses RMI in the context of building a distributed database application.

Java Management

Java management lets an application perform network administration.

Java Media

Java media creates a single API to enable developers to write rich multi-media applications interfacing with a variety of multi-media hardware devices. The Media Frameworks provides clocks for synchronizing audio, video, and MIDI. The 2D and 3D libraries provide enhanced imaging classes. The Animation API enables applications to perform transformations on 2D images. And Telephony provides an application with a single API for accessing a range of telephone devices.

Java Security

The Java security API provides developers with a simple API for enhancing applet or application security, including the ability to add cryptography, encryption, and authentication.

Java Server

Java server is Java's answer to CGI. This API allows developers to interface with and enhance Internet servers using *servlets*, executable programs that users upload to run on networks or servers.

As JavaSoft develops specific APIs, it enlists the cooperation of major industry players in the area of the API in question. In developing the database access API (the subject of this book), JavaSoft worked with a team of database leaders and listened to extensive public input. Table 1-1 shows only some of the companies who have been actively involved with the development of the database API. These companies are not simply paying lip service to the technology. They have committed time and money to make sure the level of support is intense enough to lend substance to the hype.

Table 1-1. Vendors and Partners in the Development of the Java Database API

Borland International, Inc.	Intersolv	SAS Institute Inc.
Bulletproof	Object Design	SCO
Cyber SQL Corporation	Open Horizon	Sybase
DataRamp	Open Link Software	Symantec
Dharma Systems Inc.	Oracle	Thunderstone
Gupta Corporation	Persistence Software	Visigenic Software Inc.
IBM	Presence Information Design	WebLogic Inc.
Informix	Pro-C Inc.	XDB Systems Inc.
Intersoft	RogueWave Software	Recital Corporation

The Importance of the Database

Driven by the desire for more efficient data processing, businesses have been moving to share data across departments. Small contact management databases stored in Paradox or Access databases have grown into huge multi-gigabyte distributed customer databases. International manufacturing companies are centralizing their product information databases so that internal users and Web surfers alike can view the same information. Given this volume of data being handled by corporate applications today, a serious client/server development tool needs to have a robust and simple interface for database access.

Most database systems, however, provide proprietary library calls for interfacing with them. In addition to writing code that depends on the platform of the application and the database server, we also have to use a different set of library calls for each database we wish to connect with. That certainly is not a recipe for "write once, compile once, and run anywhere." How does Java handle the closed nature of the these database engines? To fulfill Java's promise, the same application must be able to talk to any potential database engine without rewriting or recompiling.

As part of its extended APIs, Java now offers with its 1.1 release an important new way of accessing databases that addresses these portability issues and offers functionality beyond that offered by traditional client/server development tools. This database access tool is the JDBC API. This book's primary task is to talk about JDBC and show you how to use it in building client/server database applications.

Adding the Power of a Database to Java

At the time of Java's initial release, to connect a Web browser to a database over the Internet, you either had to write a CGI program or use a specialized Web-aware database that could understand SQL embedded in HTML pages. If you have ever written CGI, you certainly know that the complexity of CGI far outstretches the utility of the applications being built with it. For starters, a CGI program cannot maintain the integrity of an object-oriented system across a network, no matter what language the CGI is written in. On the client side, everything will be a simple one-dimensional HTML page. The CGI program then must spend great energy translating the information gathered by the HTML page into an object paradigm. CGI scripts are also completely incapable of doing any client-side processing, such as limiting the choices in a zip-code list box based on the state chosen. Finally, the tool most commonly used for CGI, Perl, while great for general system administration, creates programs that are a horror to maintain.

With the growing popularity of the Internet in 1995, businesses began throwing about a new term, Intranet. The Intranet is simply the part of the Internet that sits safely behind your firewall. The thrust behind the Intranet movement is not much different from Sun's motto, "the network is the computer." Specifically, an Intranet uses all of the popular Internet tools (Web browsers and servers, email, newsgroups, and so on) to let people in the same company or organization work together; it is the collaborative atmosphere of the Internet for the business tucked securely out of the reach of the chaos of the Net. While the initial release of the Java libraries made Java an ideal solution for the development of simple Intranet applets, like the ones you might find on the Web, it remained impotent as an Intranet tool without database connectivity.

The JDBC API provides the database connectivity that both Internet and Intranet developers want. With JDBC, a CGI application can be rewritten to provide interaction that is impossible under CGI. Such a Java application can maintain an object paradigm across the network. It can also provide its network resources with the database access Intranet applications demand.

How Java Interacts with a Database

Several important database concepts form the core of this book's discussion. This book assumes some basic familiarity with Java and databases. You should have a basic understanding of SQL and transaction management. Building on this foundation, we will discuss JDBC and how it can be used to execute SQL against any potential database engine.

SQL

The Java database API, JDBC, requires that the database being used support ANSI SQL-2 as the query language. The SQL language itself is worthy of a tiny mini-industry within the publishing field, and so covering it is well beyond the scope of this book. The SQL in this book, however, stays away from the more complex areas of the language and instead sticks with basic DELETE, INSERT, SELECT, and UPDATE statements.

The only additional level of complexity I use consists of stored procedures in the later chapters. Stored procedures are precompiled SQL stored on the database server and executed by naming the procedure and passing parameters to it. In other words, a stored procedure is much like a database server method. Stored procedures provide an easy mechanism for separating Java programmers from database issues and speeding up database performance.

JDBC

JDBC is a SQL-level API that allows you to embed SQL statements as arguments to methods in JDBC interfaces. To allow you to do this in a database-independent fashion, JDBC requires database vendors (like those mentioned earlier in the chapter) to furnish a run-time implementation of its interfaces. These implementations route your SQL calls to the database in the proprietary fashion it recognizes. As the programmer, though, you do not ever have to worry about how it is routing SQL statements. The facade provided by JDBC gives you complete freedom from any issues related to particular database issues—you can run the same code no matter what database is present.

Transaction management

Transaction management involves packaging related database transactions into a single unit and handling any error conditions that result. To get through this book, you need only to understand basic transaction management in the form of beginning a transaction and either committing it on success or aborting it on failure. JDBC provides you with the ability to auto-commit any transaction on the atomic level (that is, statement by statement) or to wait until a series of a statements have succeeded (or failed) and call the appropriate commit (or rollback) method.

Database Technologies

A Java client/server application can make use of one of three major database architectures:

* Relational database

* Object database

* Object-relational database

The overwhelming majority of today's database applications use relational databases. The JDBC API is thus heavily biased towards relational databases and their standard query language, SQL. Relational databases find and provide relationships about data, so they collide head on with object solutions like Java since object-oriented philosophy dictates that an object's behavior is inseparable from its data. In choosing the object-oriented reality of Java, we need to create a translation layer that maps the relational world into our object world. While JDBC provides us with access to relational databases, it leaves the issue of object-to-relational mapping up to you.

Object databases, on the other hand, do not attempt to separate object data from behavior. The best way to think of an object database is as a permanent store of objects with which your applications can interface. This object-oriented encapsulation of data, however, makes it difficult to relate data as well as relational databases do. Additionally, with JDBC so tightly bound to SQL, it is difficult to create JDBC drivers to run against an object database. As of the writing of this book, JavaSoft, in cooperation with the ODMG (Object Database Management Group), is working on a specification for a Java object database API.

Object-relational databases enjoy a "best of both worlds" advantage by providing both object and relational means of accessing data. Until recently, object relational databases have relied almost entirely on C++ objects to act as their object store. With all of the excitement around Java, however, object-relational vendors are starting to enable their systems to support database objects written and extended in Java. In this realm, our Java objects do not need to map relational data into business objects. For the sake of easy, ad-hoc querying, however, an object-relational database also provides complex relational queries; sometimes these queries can even be done in an ANSI SQL superset language.

What Java Adds to Database Programming

While the marriage of Java and database programming is beneficial to Java programmers, Java also helps database programmers. Specifically, Java provides database programmers with the following features they have traditionally lacked:

- Easy object to relational mapping
- Database independence
- Distributed computing

If you are interested in taking a pure object approach to systems development, you may have run into the cold reality that most of the world runs on relational databases into which companies have often placed hefty investments. This leaves you trying to map C++ and Smalltalk objects to relational entities. Java provides an alternative to these two tools that frees you from the proprietary interfaces associated with database programming. With the "write once, compile once, run anywhere" power that JDBC offers you, Java's database connectivity allows you to worry more about the translation of relational data into objects instead of worrying about how you are getting that data.

A Java database application does not care what its database engine is. No matter how many times the database engine changes, the application itself need never change. In addition, a company can build a class library that maps its business objects to database entities in such a way that applications do not even know whether or not their objects are being stored in a database. Later in the book I discuss building a class library that allows you to map the data you retrieve through the JDBC API into Java objects.

Java affects the way you distribute and maintain an application. A traditional client/server application requires an administrator responsible for the deployment of the client program on users' desktops. That administrator takes great pains to assure that each desktop provides a similar operating environment so that the application may run as it was intended to run. When a change is made to the application, the administrator makes the rounds and installs the upgrade.

The Java language employs the idea of the zero-install client. The object code for the entire application, client and server, resides on the network. Since the Java Virtual Machine provides an application with a guaranteed runtime environment, no administration is needed for the configuration of that environment for individual applications. The users simply use a virtual machine interface like HotJava to locate the desired application. By clicking on the application icon, a user can run it without even realizing the application was never stored on their local machine.

The traditional application makes a clear distinction among the locations where processing occurs. In traditional applications, database access occurs on the server, and GUI processing occurs on the client; the objects on the client machine talk to the database through a specialized database API. In other situations, the client might talk to the server through a set of TCP/IP or UDP/IP socket APIs. Either way, a wall of complex protocols divides the objects found on the client from those on the server. Java helps tear down this wall between client and server through another piece of its Enterprise API, Remote Method Invocation (RMI).

RMI allows applications to call methods in objects on remote machines as if those objects were located on the same machine. Calling a method in another object in Java is of course as simple as the syntax `object.method(arg)`. If you want to call that method from a remote machine without RMI, however, you would have to write code that allows you to send an object handle, method name, and arguments through a TCP/IP socket, translate it into an `object.method(arg)` call on the remote end, perform the method call, pass the return value back across the socket, and then write a bunch of code to handle network failures. That is a lot of work for a simple method call, and I did not even get into the issues we would have to deal with such as passing object references as arguments and handling garbage collection on each end. Finally, since you have written this complex protocol to handle method calls across the network, you have serious rewriting to do if you decide that a given object needs to exist on the client instead of the server (or vice versa).

With RMI, any method call, whether on the same machine or across the network, uses the same Java method call syntax. This freedom to distribute objects across the network is called a distributed object architecture. Other languages use much more complex protocols like CORBA and DCE. RMI, however, is a Java-specific

API for enabling a distributed architecture. As such, it removes many of the complexities of those two solutions.

For a client/server database application, a distributed architecture allows the various parts of the application to refer to the same physical objects when referring to particular objects in the data model. For example, take an airline ticketing system that allows customers on the Internet to book flights. Current Web applications would have a user download a bunch of flight information as an HTML page. If I book the last seat on a flight that you are viewing at the same time, you will not see my booking of that last seat. This is because on each client screen we are simply seeing copies of data from the database.

If we reconstruct this Web application so that it is using RMI to retrieve data from a single flight object on the server, we can allow any number of different customers to view the exact same plane objects at the same time. In this way, we can be certain that all viewers see any change made to the plane object simultaneously. When I book the last seat on that flight, the flight object makes an RMI call to all clients viewing it to let them know another seat was booked.

Putting It All Together

The pieces of the story are now in place. We will use JDBC for our database access, and RMI to distribute the objects that make up our application. This book covers the JDBC API in complete detail and discusses RMI as it pertains to the creation of distributed three-tier database applications. To better use these APIs once you have gone beyond this book, I strongly recommend further reading on the following topics:

- Object-oriented design methodologies
- Patterns in software development
- General database programming

2

Data and Relational Databases

> *Good sense is the most evenly shared thing in the world, for each of us thinks he is so well endowed with it that even those who are the hardest to please in all other respects are not in the habit of wanting more than they have. It is unlikely that everyone is mistaken in this. It indicates rather that the capacity to judge correctly and to distinguish true from false, which is properly what one calls common sense or reason, is naturally equal in all men, and consequently the diversity in our opinions does not spring from some of us being more able to reason than others, but only from our conducting our thoughts along different lines and not examining the same things.*
>
> —René Descartes
> *Discourse on the Method*

Before we dive into the details of database programming in Java, I would like to take a chapter to provide a basic discussion of relational databases for those of you who might have little or no experience in this area. The subject of relational databases, however, is a huge topic that cannot possibly be covered fully in this chapter. It is only designed to provide you with the most basic introduction. Experienced database developers will find nothing new in this chapter; you will probably want to skip ahead to Chapter 3.

What Is a Relational Database?

Programming is all about data processing; data is central to everything you do with a computer. Databases—like file systems—are nothing more than specialized tools for data storage. File systems are good for storing and retrieving a single volume of information associated with a single virtual location. In other words, when you want to save a WordPerfect document, a file system allows you to associate it with a location in a directory tree for easy retrieval later.

Databases provide applications with a more powerful data storage and retrieval system based on mathematical theories about data devised by Dr. E. F. Codd.

Conceptually, a relational database can be pictured as a set of spreadsheets in which rows from one spreadsheet can be related to rows from another; in reality, however, the theory behind databases is much more complex. Each "spreadsheet" in a database is called a table. As with a spreadsheet, a table is made up of rows and columns.

A simple way to illustrate the structure of a relational database is through a CD catalog. Let's say that you have decided to create a database to keep track of your music collection. Not only do you want to be able to store a list of your albums, but you also want to be able to use this data later to help you select music for parties. Your collection might look something like Table 2-1.

Table 2-1. A List of CDs from a Sample Music Collection

Artist	Title	Category	Year
The Cure	Pornography	alternative	1983
Garbage	Garbage	alternative	1996
Hole	Live Through This	alternative	1994
Nine Inch Nails	The Downward Spiral	industrial	1994
Public Image Limited	Compact Disc	alternative	1985
The Sex Pistols	Never Mind the Bullocks, Here Come the Sex Pistols	punk	1977
Skinny Puppy	Last Rights	industrial	1992
Wire	A Bell Is a Cup Until It Is Struck	alternative	1989

Of course, you could simply keep this list in a spreadsheet. But what if you wanted to have Johnny Rotten night? Nothing in this list tells you which music in your catalog features him. You might have another spreadsheet that simply lists musicians and the bands to which they belong, but there is nothing about such a spreadsheet that can provide an easy programmatic answer to your question.

With a database, you could easily ask the question "Give me all compact discs in my collection with which Johnny Rotten was involved." We will get to formally asking that question in a minute. In order to make asking that question easier, however, you have to design your database to store the information you need so that you can relate compact discs to individual musicians. We might create another table called *musicians* that stores a list of musicians. For our purposes, we will only store last name, first name, and nicknames in this list. However, we could store more information, such as the birthday. Table 2-2 shows a part of our list.

Table 2-2. The Data in the Musicians Table

Last Name	First Name	Nickname
Jourgenson	Al	
Lydon	John	Johnny Rotten
Reznor	Trent	
Smith	Robert	

Nothing in these two lists relates musicians to bands, much less musicians to compact discs. Another problem you can see in this list is that Robert Smith is a very common name and there are likely multiple artists who have that name. How do we know which Robert Smith should be related to which compact disc? Database tables generally have one or more columns called keys that uniquely identify each row. The key of the *albums* table could be the CD title; it is not uncommon, however, for the same title to be used for different albums by different bands. The simplest thing to do is to add another column to serve as the key column—let's call it an album ID. This column will just be a sequential list of numbers. As we add new discs to the collection, increment the album ID by one and insert that information. Thus album 1 is the Cure's *Pornography*, album 2 is Garbage's *Garbage*, album 3 is Hole's *Live Through This*, etc. We can also do the same thing with the musician table so that we have a musician ID for each musician.

It will now be easier to relate specific musicians to specific album titles. We still need to take a step to provide sufficient data in the proper format for us to ask our question. Specifically, we need to create a *bands* table that stores information about bands. Furthermore, we should remove each band as a column in the albums table since that information is now stored in the bands table. We are up to three tables: albums, musicians, and bands. Each table has an ID field that serves only to uniquely identify each row. The result is the data model shown in Figure 2-1.

A data model is a picture of your database tables—sometimes refered to as entities—and how they relate to one another. Our data model tells us the following things:

- Each band has one or more albums
- Each album belongs to exactly one band
- Each band contains one or more musicians
- Each musician is a member of one or more bands

This model is what is called a logical data model. A logical data model is a type of data model that tells you what you are modeling. We need to get from what we are modeling to how we are going to model it—to the physical data model. To imple-

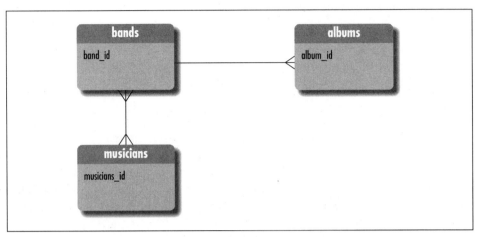

Figure 2-1. The data model for the sample compact disc database

ment this system, we need to take a few more steps. The first step is to add a column to the albums table representing the band ID for the band that produced that CD. In this way, we are relating a row in the albums table to a row in the bands table.

The complex part of our data model is the many-to-many relationship between bands and musicians. We cannot simply stick a musician ID in the bands table nor can we stick a band ID in the musicians table. This relationship is traditionally captured through something called a cross-reference table. This table, which we will call *band_musician*, contains two columns: band ID and musician ID. Unlike our other tables which represent database entities, the rows in this table represent relationships between rows in the bands and musicians tables. If John Lydon is represented by musician ID 2, the Sex Pistols are band ID 4, and Public Image Limited is band ID 5, the band_musician table would look like Table 2-3.

Table 2-3. A Portion of the band_musician Table

band_id	musician_id
3	2
4	2

An Introduction to SQL

How do we get the data into the database? And how do we get it out once it is in there? All major databases support a standard query language called SQL (which happens to stand for standard query language). SQL is not much like any programming language you might be familiar with. Instead, it is more of a structured English for talking to a database. An SQL query to the album titles from your database would look like this:

```
SELECT title FROM albums
```

In fact, much of the simplest database access comes in the form of equally simple SQL statements. Most of what you will do in SQL boils down to four SQL commands: SELECT, INSERT, UPDATE, and DELETE. You can issue SQL statements in several ways. The simplest, quickest way is through an SQL command-line tool. Each database engine comes with its own. Throughout most of this book, however, you will be sending your SQL as Java strings to JDBC methods.

NOTE   SQL keywords are case-insensitive, meaning that SELECT and se-
            lect are treated exactly the same. Depending on your database,
            however, table and column names may or may not be case-insensi-
            tive. In addition, the space between words in an SQL statement is un-
            important. You can have a newline after each word, several spaces,
            or just a single space. Throughout this book I use the convention of
            placing SQL keywords in all capitals and separating single SQL state-
            ments across multiple lines for readability.

NOTE   I should also make a couple of other syntactic notes. First, the single
            quotation mark (') is used to mark string constants and double quo-
            tation marks (") are used to show significant space, such as in col-
            umn names that contain spaces in them.

CREATE

Before we get into the four most common SQL statements, we need to actually create the tables in which our data will be stored. The major database engines provide GUI utilities that allow you to create tables without issuing any SQL. It is nevertheless good to know the SQL CREATE statement that handles the creation of database entities. Unfortunately, the exact syntax of this command is a little database dependent. The basic form is:

```
CREATE TABLE table_name (
    column_name column_type column_modifiers,
    ...,
    column_name column_type column_modifiers)
```

Using mSQL, the database engine used throughout much of this book, the musicians table might be created through the following statement:

```
CREATE TABLE musicians(
    musician_id INT,
    last_name CHAR(40),
    first_name CHAR(40),
    nickname CHAR(40))
```

The database-dependent part of the CREATE statement lies in the column modifiers. These might be things like NOT NULL, PRIMARY KEY, or other such modifiers that say something specific about the column and the kind of data it can take. You should read the SQL manual that comes with your database for specific information about column modifiers.

INSERT

With the tables in place, you use the INSERT statement to add data to them. Its form is:

```
INSERT INTO table_name(column_name, …, column_name)
VALUES (value, …, value)
```

The first column name matches to the first value you specify, the second column name to the second value you specify, and so on for as many columns as you are inserting. If you fail to specify a value for a column that is marked as NOT NULL, you will get an error on insert.

We can now add Johnny Rotten into the database using the following SQL:

```
INSERT INTO musicians(musician_id, last_name, first_name, nickname)
VALUES(2, 'Lydon', 'John', 'Johnny Rotten')
```

You have to repeat this for each row you wish to add to each table.

UPDATE

The UPDATE statement enables you to modify data that you previously inserted into the database. The UPDATE syntax looks like this:

```
UPDATE table_name
SET column_name = value,
    …,
    column_name = value
WHERE column_name = value
```

This statement introduces the WHERE clause. It is used to help identify one or more rows in the database. For example, if you had made a mistake on entering the year in which *The Downward Spiral* was released, you would issue the following statement:

```
UPDATE albums
SET year = 1994
WHERE album_id = 4
```

The WHERE column in this statement uniquely identifies the row where album_id is 4—the album ID for *The Downward Spiral*. The UPDATE statement then sets the year column to 1994 for that one row.

The WHERE clause is not limited to identifying single rows. Perhaps you want to add another music category called "old music" and set all albums older than 1980 to that category. The SQL to do that would look like this:

```
UPDATE albums
SET category = 'old music'
WHERE year < 1980
```

WARNING   You can leave out the WHERE clause of SQL commands that allow WHERE clauses. If you do this, however, your statement will operate on every relevant row. If you left out the WHERE year < 1980 in the old music example, you would make every album category change to "old music". Accidentally leaving out a WHERE clause can create disastrous results when you are using the DELETE command!

DELETE

The DELETE command looks a lot like the UPDATE statement. Its syntax is:

```
DELETE FROM table_name
WHERE column_name = value
```

Instead of changing particular values in the row, DELETE removes the entire row from the table. When you sell *The Downward Spiral*, you would therefore issue the command:

```
DELETE from albums
WHERE album_id = 4
```

SELECT

The most common SQL command you will use is the SELECT statement. It allows you to select specific rows from the database based on search criteria. It takes the following form:

```
SELECT column_name, …, column_name
```

```
FROM table_name
WHERE column_name = value
```

Retrieving all of the industrial albums from the album table would thus look like:

```
SELECT title
FROM albums
WHERE category = 'industrial'
```

Joins and Subqueries

I still have not answered the question of how you get all of the albums in which Johnny Rotten was involved. No simple SELECT following the syntax I outlined above will handle that. The SELECT statement allows you to perform some very complex queries; this is in fact the very power of a relational database. Among the more common of complex SELECT statements is the *join*. A join enables us to create a sort of virtual table on the fly that contains data from two or more tables. In the CD collection, a simple join might take the form of a search for all alternative bands:

```
SELECT bands.band_name
FROM bands, albums
WHERE albums.category = 'alternative'
    AND bands.band_id = albums.band_id
```

The newest thing you will notice here is the prefixing of table names before the column names. You need to do this since you are relating the albums and bands tables through the band_id value in both tables. In this example, we selected the names of bands from the bands table whose band ID appears in the albums table with "alternative" as a category.

But our target query is trying to relate album titles to musicians, and our data provides no direct relationship between albums and musicians. In order to accomplish this task, we need to formulate a *subquery*—a query within a query. We specifically need to select all of Johnny Rotten's bands and then get the album titles associated with those bands. Our first query is therefore the query that selects all bands associated with Johnny Rotten (musician ID 2). The main query, the one that provides us with the CD titles, uses the band IDs from the first query and selects all album titles for those band IDs:

```
SELECT title
FROM albums,
WHERE band_id IN
    (SELECT bands.band_id
     FROM bands, band_musician
     WHERE band_musician.musician_id = 2
        AND bands.band_id = band_musician.band_id)
```

Transaction Logic

A lot of times you will want to issue many updates or inserts together as part of a single transaction. When adding a new band, for example, you will want to add all of the musicians in that band together at once. Unfortunately, with many things in the computer world, individual SQL statements can fail for various reasons. The most common reason is a network problem. No matter what, you will find that errors do occur when issuing database statements; and an error in the middle of multiple related SQL statements can leave you with corrupt data.

SQL allows you to specify a set of SQL commands that are supposed to be executed together or not at all through transaction management. A transaction is basically one or more SQL statements that should be treated as a single unit of work. If one of the statements that form the transaction fails, then the whole transaction needs to be aborted, including any statements that were successfully executed up to the failure. If the whole series of statements that form the transaction succeeds, then a signal is sent to the database to make the effects of the transaction permanent.

An abort from a transaction is called a ROLLBACK, and the notification to make a transaction permanent is called a COMMIT. Some databases start off in something called auto-commit mode. In this mode, each statement is implicitly committed to the database as a complete transaction as it is sent to the database. If you are not in auto-commit mode, the database waits for you to send an explicit COMMIT or ROLLBACK. If you send a COMMIT, any changes you made are reflected in the database permanently. A ROLLBACK, however, returns the database to its state after the last COMMIT.

Transaction logic will be fully illustrated in Chapters 4 and 5.

3

Foundations for an Object-Oriented Database Application

Each thing is, as it were, in a space of possible states of affair. This space I can imagine as empty, but I cannot imagine the thing without the space.
—Ludwig Wittgenstein
Tractatus Logico Philosophicus

In isolation, your Java objects have no meaning—they do nothing. Java objects represent things outside the application: a customer, a savings account, and so on. Before getting into the details of individual objects, we truly need to understand the space in which we expect them to operate. In this chapter, we will be laying the foundations for database development in the object-oriented world of Java by examining the architecture of an application we will be building over the course of this book. We will not touch JDBC or RMI or any of the other details required for creating individual objects. My goal here is instead to help you cut down on the work you will need do over and over again each time you build a database application. The classes I show you in this chapter are common and generic, perhaps something that you could use to create a standard package for use in all kinds of applications.

One thing you may have noticed about Java or similar object-oriented languages like Smalltalk or Python is that there are so many classes. You want to try to understand what class X does, but you find that it in turn extends class Z, which contains classes A and B. If you are totally comfortable with the object-oriented paradigm, this interweaving of classes may not faze you. On the other hand, it is very easy for it to seem confusing to people accustomed to dealing with languages like C. Unlike C, where you may have a library function and perhaps an associated data structure, Java bundles up data and functions inside classes for manipulating that data. Java data never gets directly manipulated except by the class that owns the data.

I will of course continue operating in Java's object-oriented framework. Among other things, this means that wherever we need to represent a new concept, we will use new classes. You should approach each new class trying to understand what class it extends, which interfaces it implements, and what others it relates to in other ways. I will try to help you along graphically wherever possibly by providing object models that illustrate the object relationships.

Client/Server Development

Client/server is an application architecture that divides processing among two or more processes, often on two or more machines. Any database application is a client/server application that handles data storage and retrieval in the database process and data manipulation and presentation somewhere else. The server is the database engine that stores the data, and the client is the process that gets or creates the data. The idea behind the client/server architecture in a database application is of course to provide multiple users with access to the same data.

The simplest shape a client/server architecture will take is called a *two-tier* architecture. The term "two-tier" describes the way in which application processing can be divided in a client/server application. A two-tier application ideally provides multiple workstations with a uniform presentation layer that communicates with a centralized data storage layer. The presentation layer is generally the client, and the data storage layer is the server. Some exceptional environments, such as the X Window System, shuffle around the roles of client and server.

Most Internet applications—email, telnet, ftp, gopher, and even the Web—are simple two-tier applications. Without providing a lot of data interpretation or processing, these applications provide a simple interface to access information across the Internet. When most application programmers write their own client/server applications, they tend to follow this two-tier structure.

Figure 3-1 shows how two-tier systems give clients access to centralized data. If we use the Web as an example, the Web browser on the client side retrieves data stored at a Web server.

Strengths and Limitations of a Two-Tier Architecture

The architecture of a system depends on the application. For situations such as the display of simple Web pages, we do not need anything more than a two-tier design has to offer. This is because the display of static HTML pages requires very little data manipulation, and thus there is very little to fight over. The server sends the page as a stream of text, and the client formats it based on the HTML tags. There are none of the complicating factors we will see in upcoming applications:

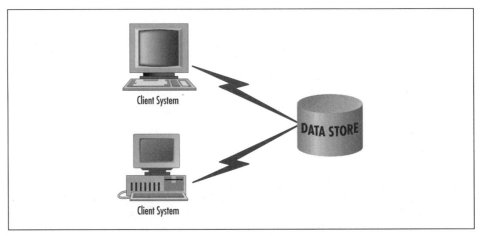

Figure 3-1. The two-tier client/server architecture

choices between different tasks, redirecting of tasks to subordinate methods, searches through distributed databases, and so on.

Even when your application gets slightly more complex—such as a simple data-entry application like the many Web-based contests popping up on the Internet—a two-tier architecture still makes sense. Let's look at how we might build such an application to see why additional complexity is unnecessary. Figure 3-2 shows this application in the context of a two-tier architecture that we saw in Figure 3-1.

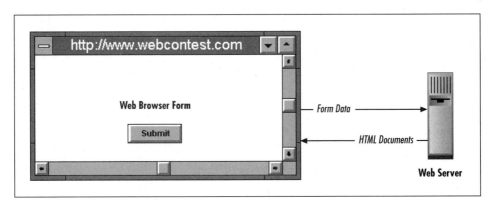

Figure 3-2. A contest registration application using a two-tier architecture

In addition to displaying the HTML forms we receive from the server, our client also accepts user input and sends it back to the server for storage. You might even build in some batch processing on the server to validate a contest entry and reject any ineligible ones. The application really requires no additional processing in order to do its job.

The application can easily handle all its processing between the client and server; nothing calls for an additional layer. But what if the application were even more complex? Let's say that instead of waiting for ineligible entries to be submitted before rejecting them, we filter out ineligible entries on the client so people are not forced to fill out a form only to be rejected. In place of handling entry processing in a separate application, we now need to write logic somewhere that will reject these rogue entries. Where are we going to do it?

Without Java, a client-side scripting language like JavaScript, or some peculiar browser plug-in, you can forget handling this processing on the client side. Processing in a Web browser can happen using only one of those three solutions. The browser plug-in solution is very unlikely since it requires the user to download and install a foreign application simply for the sake of filling out a one-time entry into a contest. Browser scripting languages, on the other hand, lack Java's portability and its ability to cleanly interface with server systems. The enterprise solution is Java.

Using Java on the client, we can preserve the simple two-tier architecture. This solution is great if our processing is limited to simple data validation (Is your birthday a real date? Did you enter all the required fields?). But what if we add even more complexity? Now we will require the application to be a generic contest entry application that we can sell to multiple companies running Internet contests. One of the implications of this generic design is that our application must be able to adapt to contests having different entry eligibility rules. If our eligibility rules are located in a Java applet on the client that is talking directly to the database, then changing eligibility rules essentially means rewriting the application! In addition, our direct database access ties our application to the same data model without regard for the individuality of the different contests the application is supposed to serve. Our needs have now outstripped the abilities of our two-tier architecture.

The Problem of the Fat Client

Perhaps you have seen the sort of scope-creep in a single application in the way I introduced new functions into the contest application. Ideally, the client/server architecture is supposed to let each machine do only the processing relevant to its specialization. Workstations are designed to provide users with a graphical interface, so they do data presentation. Servers are designed to handle complex data and networking management, so they serve as the data stores. But as systems get more complex, more needs appear that have no clear place in the two-tier model.

This evolution of application complexity has been paralleled by opposing trends in hardware. Client machines have grown larger and more powerful; server machines have scaled down and become less expensive. While client machines have been able to keep up with the more complex user interface needs, servers have becomes less capable of handling more complex data storage needs. Where a single mainframe once handled a company's most complex databases, you might find today the same databases distributed across dozens of smaller servers. As odd as this sounds, companies do this because it is immensely cheaper to buy a dozen small workstations than to buy one mainframe. Financial pressures have thus pushed new processing needs onto the client, leading to what is commonly called the problem of the "fat client."

Two-tier, fat-client systems are notorious for their inability to adapt to changing environments and scale with growing user and data volume. Even though a client's primary task is the presentation of data, a fat client is loaded with knowl- edge completely unrelated to that task. What happens if you need to distribute your data across multiple databases or across multiple servers? What happens if some small bit of business logic changes? You have to modify, test, and redis- tribute a client program whose core functionality has nothing to do with the changes you made.

The Problem of Object Reuse

Object reuse is a very vague but central concept in object-oriented development. We all know it is a *good thing*, but we can have some very different things in mind when we speak of it. In one very common sense, object reuse is simply code reuse. The code we used to build application X, we used in building application Y. But in another sense, object reuse means using exactly the same object *instances* in one application that we are using in another application. For instance, the customer account objects you likely built for an ATM system could be used by a new Web interface you are building. While a two-tier system can do contortions to achieve the former sense of object reuse, it almost never can achieve the latter.

In the simplest form of object reuse, we would like to take code developed for one application, rewrite small bits of it, and have it run with minimal work. Two-tier solutions have had a nasty time doing this because they are so closely tied to the database. In PowerBuilder, for example, your GUI objects map directly to tables in a database! You need to throw away a large chunk of your GUI when moving from one environment to the next. Some very clever people—including a few I have worked with—have built some complex class libraries to work around this problem. But my experience has been that such systems lack the flexibility we want in a toolkit of reusable objects.

Source code reuse is not the real object reuse we are looking for. We want to reuse actual object instances. If you are looking at building a system for viewing bank accounts both from the Web and from an ATM machine, you really want the user's Web browser and the ATM machine to be looking at the exact same data, especially if they are looking at that data at the same instant. Doing this with a two-tier system is nearly impossible since each client ends up with its own copy of the data. When one client changes some data, other clients end up with old data, resulting in a problem called dirty writes. A dirty write is a situation in which someone tries to modify data based on an old, out-of-date copy of the database. If my spouse at an ATM makes a withdrawal while I am paying bills at home, I want to see that change happen. If we each are looking at copies of the original data, however, I will end up paying a bill with money that my spouse just withdrew!

If a client, on the other hand, is simply observing objects located in some central-ized location, it is always dealing with the most recent information. When my spouse withdraws that last $100, my Web browser is immediately notified so that I do not act on stale information. Java makes things easier for us by providing observer and observable classes; later in this chapter I'll show how to apply them to the database problems I've introduced here.

When to Use a Two-Tier Design

Two-tier solutions do have a place in client/server development. Simple applica-tions with immediate deadlines that do not require a lot of maintenance are perfect for a two-tier architecture. The following checklist provides important questions to ask before committing yourself to a two-tier design. If you can answer 'yes' to each of the questions in the checklist, then a two-tier architecture is likely your best solution. Otherwise you might consider a three-tier design.

- Does your application use a single database?
- Is your database engine located on a single CPU?
- Is your database likely to stay approximately the same size over time?
- Is your user base likely to stay approximately the same size over time?
- Are your requirements fixed with little or no possibility of change?
- Do you expect minimal maintenance after you deliver the application?

Adding a Third Tier

We can avoid the problems of the previous section by extending the two tiers to three. A three-tier architecture adds to the two-tier model a new layer that isolates data processing in a central location and maximizes object reuse. Figure 3-3 shows how this new third layer might fit into an application architecture.

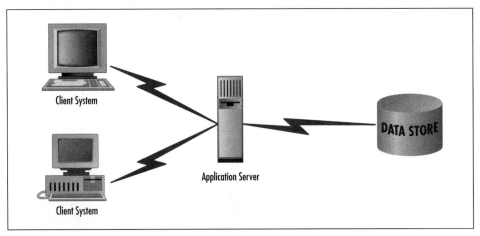

Figure 3-3. A three-tier architecture

Isolated Database Connectivity

I've already mentioned that JDBC frees us from concerns related to portability among proprietary database APIs. Unfortunately, it does not (and it could not) provide us with a means to liberate our applications from our data model. If your application uses JDBC in a two-tier environment, it is still talking directly to the database. Any change in the database ends up costing you a change in the presentation layer.

To avoid this extra cost, we should isolate our database connection so that our presentation does not care anything about the way we store our data. We can take advantage of Java's object-oriented nature and create a system in which our clients talk only to objects on the server. Database connectivity becomes an issue hidden within each server object. Suddenly, the presentation layer stops caring about where the database is, as well as if we are even using a database at all. The client only sees middle-tier objects.

Centralized Data Processing

The middle tier of a three-tier architecture—the application server—handles those data processing issues we have found out of place in either of the other tiers. The application server is populated by problem-specific objects commonly called business objects. Returning to the banking application, our business objects are things like accounts, customers, and transactions that exist independently of how a user might see them. An account, for example, is concerned with processing new banking transactions. It does not care whether an ATM machine is viewing it, a teller is viewing it at his or her console, or the bank is planning to allow users to access it from the Web. An application server layer will generally consist of a data store interface and a public API.

The data store interface is hidden from external objects. Internally, a business object has methods to save it to and restore it from a database. Information about how this happens is not available outside the object, and thus does not affect other objects. On the other hand, the business object does provide a limited, public interface to allow external objects access to it. In a two-tier application, our GUI would have displayed account information directly from the database. In a three-tier system, however, the GUI learns everything about an account from an account business object instead of from the database. If the GUI wants to know something it should not be allowed to know, the business object can prevent it. Similarly, if the GUI wants to make a change to that object, it submits that change to the object instead of to the database.

These centralized rules for processing data inside business objects are called business rules. No matter what your problem domain is, the rules for how data should be processed rarely change. For example, no matter what application talks to our account objects, that application should not (unfortunately) allow you to write checks for money you do not have. It is a rule that governs the way the bank does business. A three-tier architecture allows us to use the same exact business rules across all applications that operate on our business objects.

Business Object Presentation

User interfaces are very ephemeral things. They change constantly in the development process as users experiment with them; their final appearance depends heavily on the hardware being used, the application's user base, and the purpose of the application in question. The presentation layer of a three-tier application should therefore contain only user interface code that can easily be modified on a whim.

Our banking application could use any of these different presentation layers:

- The teller window's console at the bank
- The ATM machine
- The Web applet

Figure 3-4 shows how we intend to present an account from a teller PC.

Database vendors know that data presentation is a central requirement, and they have developed some fancy solutions for creating GUIs. The good ones are easy to use and produce nice-looking results, but since they are based on a two-tiered vision they allow rules and decision-making to leak into the presentation layer. For instance, take PowerBuilder, which has been on the leading edge of designing

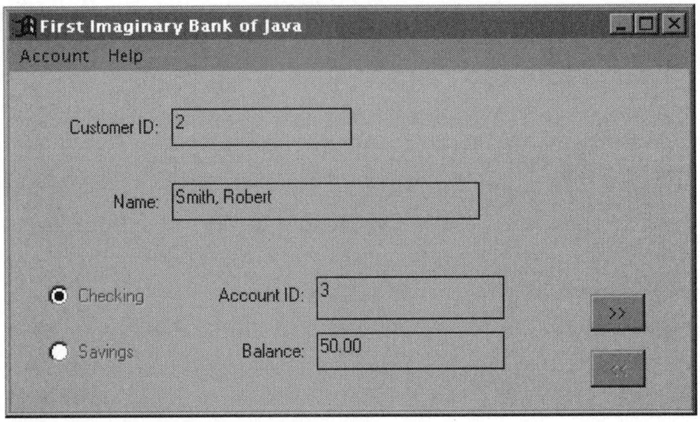

Figure 3-4. An account as viewed from the teller console

a rapid application development environment for building database front-ends. It uses GUI objects called DataWindows to map relational data into a graphical user interface display. With a Datawindow, you can use simple drag-and-drop to associate a database column with a particular GUI widget.

Because a Datawindow maps the user interface directly to the database, it does not work well in a three-tier system where you are mapping the user interface to intermediary business objects. We will, however, create a user interface library in Chapter 7 that captures the Datawindow level of abstraction in a way that better suits a three-tier distributed architecture. Instead of mapping rows from a database to a display area on a user interface, we will create a one-to-one mapping of business objects to specific GUI views of them. Figure 3-5 contrasts these two approaches.

Object Patterns

Patterns are recurring forms in software development that we can capture at a low level and reuse across very dissimilar applications. Within any application scope are problems we have all encountered before; patterns are the result of our recognizing those common problems and creating a common solution.

The first step to identifying the design patterns is to identify problems in generic terms. We already know that we need to relate GUI widgets on the client to business objects in the application server. In other words, we want to create GUI widgets that observe changes in centralized business objects. We also know that we need to make those business objects persistent by saving them to a database. We should therefore take a look at a few common patterns that will help accomplish these goals.

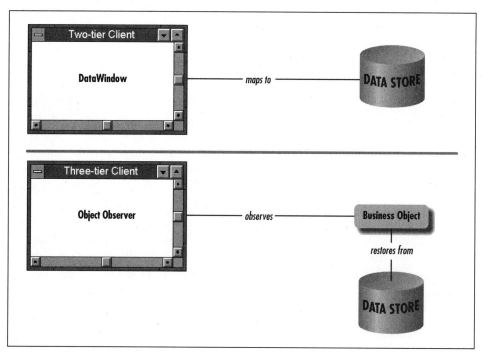

Figure 3-5. Two-tier Datawindows versus three-tier access

The Observer Pattern

The observer pattern captures situations in which one object is interested in changes that occur in another. The first object, the *observer*, is therefore said to be observing the second object, the *observable*. The Java AWT uses this pattern through its `ImageObserver` interface. When you create an image, it takes time for the image to load and be ready for drawing. Of course, you do not want your application to sit around and wait for the image to be loaded—you could be doing valuable things in another thread while the image is being loaded. Fortunately, the AWT spawns off a special thread for loading the image and lets you do other application processing. You are left with the challenge of finding out when the image is done loading so that you can draw it on the GUI.

An `ImageObserver` is any component that indicates it cares about changes in an `Image` object. When your application calls `getImage()`, it can pass as a final argument an object that will observe the created image. This object implements `ImageObserver` and does whatever your application needs to do (like drawing the image) once the loading of the image is complete.

Returning to the banking application, my spouse at the ATM machine can withdraw money from a checking account that I am looking at it on the Web. If the

GUI widgets in my applet are not actively observing those accounts, they will not know that my account has less money than it did a minute ago. If the application uses the observer pattern, however, any time a change occurs in the checking account, both the ATM machine and the Web browser get notified.

Java provides two classes in the `java.util` library designed to implement this pattern. `java.util.Observer` is a Java interface that requires implementers to define a method called `update()`. Whenever an object being observed by the observer object changes, it calls this `update()` method to notify the observer of the change. Conversely, the `java.util.Observable` class provides inheriting classes with methods for tracking observers and notifying them of changes. Objects interested in observing an observable object call the observable's `add-Observer()` method. Any time a change in which the observer might be interested occurs, the observable object calls its `notifyObservers()` method. The `notifyObservers()` method implemented in `java.util.Observable` calls the `update()` method in all of its observers with the event information you pass as an argument to the method. Figure 3-6 shows how an observer interacts with the object it is observing.

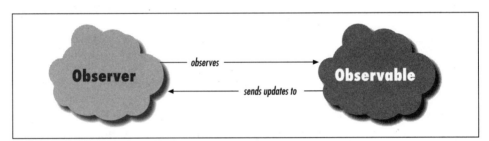

Figure 3-6. The observer relationship as implemented in the Java API

Observing objects across a network is a non-trivial problem. To do it right, you need some tool for triggering methods in remote objects. Later in the book, I will introduce you to Remote Method Invocation (RMI) and show how it can be used to enable communication among distributed objects.

The Persistence Pattern

To some degree or another, most applications are concerned about some sort of persistence. Persistence is simply the ability to have information from an application instance exist for later instances of the application (or even other applications) to use. An object-oriented database application uses a database to enable its business objects to exist beyond the traditional object life-cycle. We want our customer object to exist at least as long as the customer exists. We want the accounts to exist at least as long as they are open. The persistence pattern solves this problem by creating a single interface for any potential method of extending an object's life.

The simplest implementation of object persistence is the creation of flat files. Each time an object changes, it saves itself to a file. When your application re-creates it later on, it then goes back to that file and restores itself. While this sort of persistence is useful for small systems, it is extremely inefficient and does not scale at all for big systems.

Another backend tool for object persistence is the relational database. Here we have arrived at our goal. Instead of saving to a file with each change in an object, our objects update the database. Although saving to a database is a lot different from saving to a file, the same basic concepts of saving, restoring, committing, and aborting apply to both. What differs is the system-dependent specifics; for instance, you execute a simple file write for a file save, but an SQL UPDATE for a database save. We can therefore write a generic persistence interface that provides a single set of methods for persistence regardless of whether you are using a data-base or flat files. Your business objects never care how they are being saved, so the business logic just calls a save() method and allows a persistence-specific class to handle how that saving is implemented.

The persistence pattern defines an interface that prescribes these four basic behaviors:

abort()
   An abort returns the object to its state prior to the last save attempt.

remove()
   A remove flags the object to be deleted from the data store at the next save.

restore()
   A restore tells the object to load its data from the data store.

save()
   A save operation attempts to save any changes made to the object to the data store.

Java allows you to write different classes that implement the same interface. Because of the complex behavior of some patterns, like the persistence pattern, an abstract class makes more sense than a simple interface. In order to maintain the flexibility to add different mechanisms for persistence without rewriting code, this class library uses the peer pattern in order to implement the persistence pattern.

The Peer Pattern

You have probably noticed something called the peer pattern in the `java.awt` package. The peer pattern enables you to encapsulate the details of a particularly complex set of behaviors in a separate class. In the `java.awt` package, the Java library hides all of the details of GUI implementation within GUI component peers. The high-level Java component you manipulate in your code takes upon itself functions like remembering that a user has clicked on it—functions that do not depend on the underlying platform-specific implementation. The component passes on to its peer those functions that require an understanding of the underlying platform, like how to change color in response to a user click. As a GUI developer, this provides you with a single API for writing windowing code that will port to any Java Virtual Machine, while also hiding the details of each individual Java Virtual Machine from the more generic Java classes.

Why hide a window's implementation details from itself? If JavaSoft wrote platform-specific code inside the `Frame` class, for instance, they would have faced a terrible tangle when they ported it to a new platform, such as moving from Windows to the Macintosh. Instead of cleanly stripping out and replacing one class, they would have had to touch thousands of lines of code that handle generic interface issues.

Similarly, our business objects have quite a bit of functionality, only a portion of which is persistence. While we could write JDBC code inside our business objects, we would lose the encapsulation that putting the JDBC persistence inside a peer would give us. We will thus use database peers to provide persistence for our business objects.

The Factory Pattern

Another common pattern found in the core Java libraries is the factory pattern. This pattern encapsulates the creation of objects inside a single interface. The Java 1.1 internationalization support is peppered with factory classes. The `java.util.ResourceBundle` class, for example, contains logic that allows you to find a bundle of resources for a specific locale without having to know which subclass of `ResourceBundle` is the right one to instantiate. A `Resource-Bundle` is an object that might contain translations of error messages, menu item labels, and text labels for your application. By using a `ResourceBundle`, you can create an application that will appear in French to French users, German to German users, and English to English users.

Because of the factory pattern, using a `ResourceBundle` is quite easy. To create a save button, for example, you might have the following code:

```
bundle b = ResourceBundle.getBundle(Locale.getDefault());
button b = new Button(b.getString("SAVE"));
```

This code actually uses two factory methods: `Locale.getDefault()` and `ResourceBundle.getBundle()`. `Locale.getDefault()` constructs a `Locale` instance representing the locale in which your application is being run. For a French user, this `Locale` instance would represent France and the French language. For a German, on the other hand, it would represent Germany and the German language. The `ResourceBundle.getBundle()` method in turn finds a `ResourceBundle` instance that supports the language and customs for that locale. The French `ResourceBundle` will thus return "Enregistrer" for the `getString()` call and the English one would return "Save".

The goal of the factory pattern is to capture the creation logic of certain objects in one method. The benefit of providing a single location for the creation of certain objects is that you can handle any rules regarding the creation of those objects in that once. If you use new everywhere, however, a change in business rules will require a change and retest of every single new in your code.

There are actually two types of factory patterns: abstract factories and concrete factories. Concrete and abstract factories differ simply in the kind of objects they create: you write a concrete factory to instantiate objects of a class name known to you at compile time, whereas you write an abstract factory to determine at runtime what sort of object to instantiate. One place we could use the latter in the banking application is to determine at runtime what type of account to instantiate. In this case, account type is simply a field in the database, "C" for checking, "S" for savings. While both account types have the same data structure, different rules apply to each, so we need different classes to represent them. We can use an abstract factory to determine if a savings account or checking account object should be created based on the data from the database.

Business Patterns

In addition to generic patterns, we also want to look for patterns specific to the type of application being built. For example, we might build our banking application generic enough so that we could easily adapt it to the rules of any bank. After all, no matter what bank you use, your account has a balance, you can deposit into it, withdraw from it, etc. By encapsulating the essence of what it is to be a bank account in an account super-class, you can adapt application specific rules in inheriting classes without reinventing the wheel each time you build a banking application.

A Persistence Library

So far in this chapter we have been discussing some of the high-level concepts behind three-tier client/servers in an object-oriented environment. I am going to switch gears now and talk about how we should go about building such a client/server application. The first task is to design a persistence library that we can use in any database application. After that, we will design the actual banking application that will use this persistence library.

Figure 3-7 is an object model for a reusable class library for building applications using persistent objects. This library will form the core of our banking application by providing a persistence interface for our business objects.

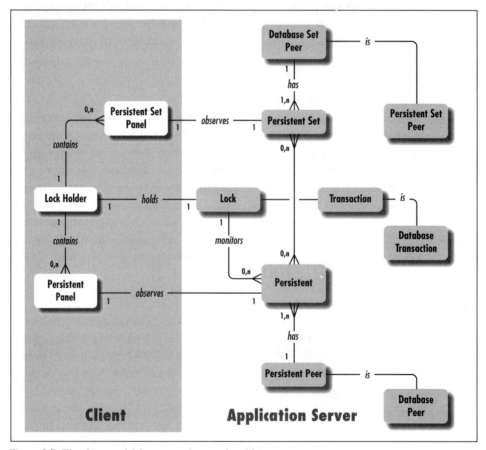

Figure 3-7. The object model for our persistence class library

There is a lot going on in this object model. As with any object model, we want to provide a snapshot of the objects that should appear in the system. Wherever two objects interact with each other, anywhere from one to many lines connects them, depending on whether the relationship is one-to-one or one-to-many. You should not be overly concerned with understanding everything that is going on here right now; we discuss each of the objects in detail over the course of the book.

These classes together provide the following functionality:

- They isolate database-specific functionality in a handful of peer classes.

- They provide a single focal point for transaction management.

- They provide business objects with an interface that is independent of the back-end used for object persistence.

Most business objects in our application are persistent objects. A persistent object is responsible for defining the behaviors we identified for the persistence pattern. Specifically, a persistent object is capable of saving itself, restoring itself, and deleting itself in addition to aborting any of those operations. When the ATM application needs to save changes to my savings account, it just tells the savings account to save itself. The `Persistent` interface prescribes the methods that persistent objects implement in order to perform those persistence operations.

Because we do not want any code specific to database persistence in the account, we cannot simply implement those `Persistent` methods by writing database code. The `PersistentPeer` class defines an interface to be implemented by technology-specific classes. In our library, we have a `DatabasePeer` class, which implements the `PersistentPeer` methods using JDBC. Similarly, we could also implement the `PersistentPeer` interface in a `FilePeer` class that uses file I/O for persistence.

Most applications need the ability to retrieve persistent objects in groups that have something in common. When I log in to my bank account from the Web, for example, the applet will probably want to grab a list of all of my accounts. The `PersistentSet` class keeps track of persistent objects associated with a given query result set. For example, when the application asks the database for all of my accounts, it needs something other than a persistent object for finding the matching accounts. The banking application could thus create an `AccountSet` class that extends `PersistentSet` and provides a mechanism for getting a list of accounts for a given customer.

Because you may need to save multiple persistent objects in the same database transaction, you need something to help manage the success or failure of individual object saves in the context of a single transaction. The `Transaction` class from Figure 3-7 manages the transaction logic behind all persistence operations. When the application wants to save my accounts after I have transferred money from my checking account to my savings account, it tells the `Transaction` for my accounts to perform a save. The `Transaction` in turn tells each account to save itself. If an error occurs saving any one of the accounts, the `Transaction` goes back and tells each account to abort the save.

Figure 3-8 diagrams the flow of persistence processing in an application using this architecture.

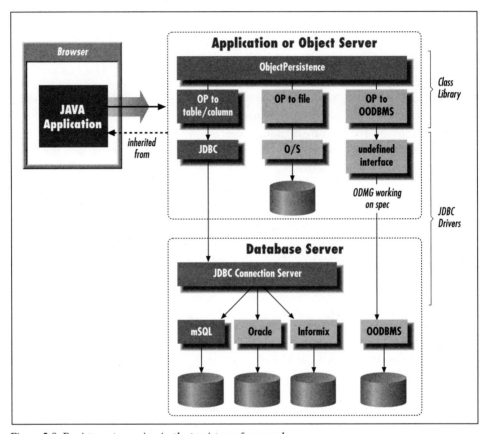

Figure 3-8. Persistence processing in the persistence framework

The Banking Application Design

Before we can build a banking application that demonstrates the Java database access concepts in this book, we should take a moment to understand exactly what we will be building. Our goal is to build a banking application that allows multiple diverse clients to view the same exact banking information at the same time. When account information changes, any clients viewing that information should see the change immediately.

Application Requirements

- The banking application will manage the creation, maintenance, and closing of customer accounts.

- Users include customers and tellers who may perform account transactions through ATM machines, teller consoles, or the World Wide Web.

- For simplicity's sake, we are handling only two types of accounts: checking accounts and savings accounts.

- Checking accounts may dip into any associated savings accounts to cover overdrafts.

- For checking accounts with associated savings accounts, the customer must have enough money combined in all accounts to cover any overdrafts.

The Object Model

From the requirements, we can identify the objects pictured in Figure 3-9, our object model.

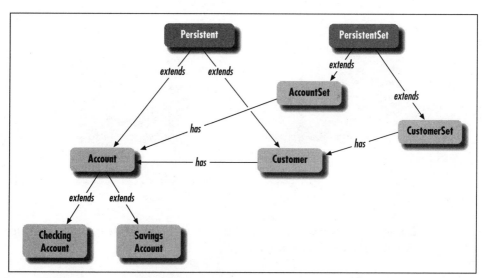

Figure 3-9. The banking application object model

I have kept this object model as simple as possible so we can concentrate on the task of using Java in a database application. It is certainly not capable of supporting a real banking system. Nevertheless, this object model captures the essence of tracking bank accounts related to individual customers.

The persistent objects at the heart of this system are the savings and checking accounts, customers, and tellers. The user interacts with these business objects using one of three GUIs. For now, we are leaving the GUI out of the design. We address GUI issues in Chapter 7. However, right now we need to know that the GUIs will allow a user—a customer or a teller—to log in to the system as well as view and modify the business objects.

One particular relationship worth noting is an `Account` with its subclasses `SavingsAccount` and `CheckingAccount`. The `Account` class maintains all of the attributes of bank accounts, while the subclasses handle the different rules associated with the different kinds of accounts. For `SavingsAccount`, there are no special rules in this application. `CheckingAccount`, on the other hand, has to be able to search through the customer's savings accounts to cover any overdrafts.

The Data Model

Because we are using a relational database to provide persistence for the application, we need a data model to show how the database should be structured.

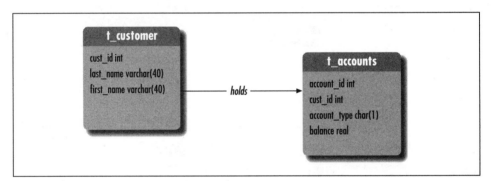

Figure 3-10. The banking application data model

In Chapter 6, we use this data model and the peer classes from the object model to show how JDBC provides Java with an interface for database access.

4

Database Access Through JDBC

These common thoughts are expressed in a shared public language, consisting of shared signs ... a sign has a "sense" that fixes the reference and is "grasped by everybody" who knows the language...

—Noam Chomsky
Language and Thought

Database programming has traditionally been a technological Tower of Babel. We are faced with dozens of available database products, and each one talks to our applications in its own private language. If your application needs to talk to a new database engine, you have to teach it (and yourself) a new language. As Java programmers, however, we should not be worrying about such translation issues. Java is supposed to bring us the ability to "write once, compile once, and run anywhere," so it should bring it to us with database programming as well.

Java's JDBC API gives us a shared language through which our applications can talk to database engines. Following in the tradition of its other multi-platform APIs such as the AWT, JDBC provides us with a set of interfaces that create a common point at which database applications and database engines can meet. In this chapter, we will discuss the basic interfaces that JDBC provides.

What Is JDBC?

Working with leaders in the database field, JavaSoft developed a single API for database access—JDBC. As part of this process, they kept three main goals in mind:

- JDBC should be an SQL-level API.

41

- JDBC should capitalize on the experience of existing database APIs.

- JDBC should be simple.

An SQL-level API means that JDBC allows us to construct SQL statements and embed them inside Java API calls. In short, you are basically using SQL. But JDBC lets you smoothly translate between the world of the database and the world of the Java application. Your results from the database, for instance, are returned as Java variables, and access problems get thrown as exceptions. Later on in the book, we go a step further and talk about how we can completely hide the existence of the database from a Java application using a database class library.

Because of the confusion caused by the proliferation of proprietary database access APIs, the idea of a universal database access API to solve this problem is not a new one. In fact, JavaSoft drew upon the successful aspects of one such API, Open DataBase Connectivity (ODBC). ODBC was developed to create a single standard for database access in the Windows environment. Although the industry has accepted ODBC as the primary means of talking to databases in Windows, it does not translate well into the Java world. First of all, ODBC is a C API that requires intermediate APIs for other languages. But even for C developers, ODBC has suffered from an overly complex design that has made its transition outside of the controlled Windows environment a failure. ODBC's complexity arises from the fact that complex, uncommon tasks are wrapped up in the API with its simpler and more common functionality. In other words, in order for you to understand a little of ODBC, you have to understand a lot.

In addition to ODBC, JDBC is heavily influenced by existing database programming APIs such as X/OPEN SQL Call Level Interface. JavaSoft wanted to re-use the key abstractions from these APIs, which would ease acceptance by database vendors and capitalize on the existing knowledge capital of ODBC and SQL CLI developers. In addition, JavaSoft also realized that deriving an API from existing ones can provide quick development of solutions for database engines that support the old protocols. Specifically, JavaSoft worked in parallel with Intersolv to create an ODBC bridge that maps JDBC calls to ODBC calls, thus giving Java applications access to any database management system (DBMS) that supports ODBC.

JDBC attempts to remain as simple as possible while providing developers with maximum flexibility. A key criterion employed by JavaSoft is simply asking whether database access applications read well. The simple and common tasks use simple interfaces, while more uncommon or bizarre tasks are enabled through extra interfaces. For example, three interfaces handle a vast majority of database access. JDBC nevertheless provides several other interfaces for handling more complex and unusual tasks.

The Structure of JDBC

JDBC accomplishes its goals through a set of Java interfaces, each implemented differently by individual vendors. The set of classes that implement the JDBC interfaces for a particular database engine is called a JDBC driver. In building a database application, you do not have to think about the implementation of these underlying classes at all; the whole point of JDBC is to hide the specifics of each database and let you worry about just your application. Figure 4-1 shows the JDBC classes and interfaces.

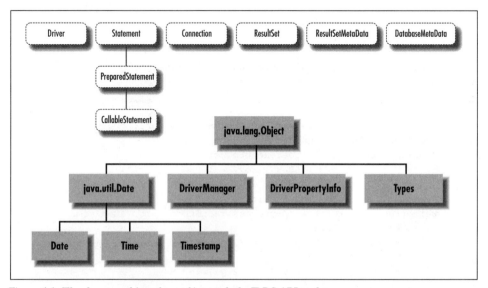

Figure 4-1. The classes and interfaces of java.sql, the JDBC API package

If you think about a database query for any database engine, it requires you to connect to the database, issue your SELECT statement, and process the result set. In Example 4-1, we have the full code listing for a simple SELECT application from the Imaginary JDBC Driver for mSQL.* I wrote this driver for the Center for Imaginary Environments (*http://www.imaginary.com*), which is a non-commercial organization that promotes the development of virtual environment technologies like muds. This application is a single class that gets all of the rows from a table in an mSQL database located on my Sun box. First, it connects to the database by getting a database connection under my user id, borg, from the JDBC Driver-Manager class. It uses that database connection to create a Statement object

---

* mSQL stands for Mini-SQL. It is a small database that supports a subset of SQL and is ideal for systems that need a database that can operate with few system resources. You can get more information on it at *http://Hughes.com.au.*

that performs the SELECT query. A ResultSet object then provides the application with the key and val fields from the t_test table.

Example 4-1. A Simple SELECT Application from the Imaginary JDBC Implementation for mSQL

```
import java.sql.*;

public class SelectApp {
  public static void main(String args[]) {
    String url = "jdbc:msql://athens.imaginary.com:4333/db_web";

    try {
      Class.forName("imaginary.sql.iMsqlDriver");
    }
    catch( Exception e ) {
      System.out.println("Failed to load mSQL driver.");
      return;
    }
    try {
      Connection con = DriverManager.getConnection(url, "borg", "");
      Statement select = con.createStatement();
      ResultSet result = select.executeQuery
                          ("SELECT key, val FROM t_test");

      System.out.println("Got results:");
      while(result.next()) { // process results one row at a time
        int key = result.getInt(1);
        String val = result.getString(2);

        System.out.println("key = " + key);
        System.out.println("val = " + val);
      }
      select.close();
      con.close();
    }
    catch( Exception e ) {
      e.printStackTrace();
    }
  }
}
```

If you already have Java experience, then you should be able to understand the flow of the code in Example 4-1 without knowing any JDBC. There are no references to specific database engine classes. Instead, the code simply uses JDBC interfaces to provide a facade for the DBMS-specific implementation. The JDBC implementation, in turn, performs the actual database access somewhere behind the scenes.

In this simple application, the `SelectApp` class asks the JDBC `DriverManager` to hand it the proper database implementation based on a database URL. The database URL looks similar to other Internet URLs. The actual content of the URL is loosely specified as *jdbc:subprotocol:subname*. The subprotocol identifies which driver to use, and the subname provides the driver with any required connection information. For the Imaginary JDBC Implementation for mSQL that I used in testing the above example, the URL is *jdbc:msql://athens.imaginary.com:4333/db_web*. In other words, this URL says to use the mSQL JDBC driver to connect to the database db_web on the server running at port 4333 on *athens.imaginary.com*. Each URL, however, is specific to the JDBC implementation being sought, and so I can't say anything more explicit about it. Whatever its format, the primary function of a database URL is to uniquely identify the implementation needed by the application and pass that implementation any information it needs in order to connect to the proper database.

Databases and Drivers

In putting together the examples in this book, I used both an mSQL database for the simple Chapter 4 examples and an Oracle database for the more complex examples of Chapter 5. If you do not have a corporate pocketbook to back up your database purchase, mSQL is probably the most feasible solution. You should keep in mind, however, that mSQL does not allow you to abort transactions and does not support the stored procedures used in Chapter 5. Whatever your database choice, you must set up your database engine, create a database, and create the tables shown in the Chapter 3 data model before you can begin writing JDBC code.

Once your database engine is installed and your database is all set up, you will need a JDBC driver for that database engine. You can find an mSQL JDBC driver at *http://www.imaginary.com/Java*. The more commercial database engines like Oracle have commercial JDBC drivers. Most of them, however, allow you to have a free trial period for experimenting with the driver. Follow the install instructions for the driver you choose, and remember that some JDBC drivers require to you install native code on client machines. To help you understand what different drivers require, JavaSoft has defined the following driver categorization system:

type 1

These drivers use a bridging technology to access a database. The JDBC-ODBC bridge that comes with the JDK 1.1 is a good example of this kind of driver. It provides a gateway to the ODBC API. Implementations of that API in turn do the actual database access. Bridge solutions generally require software to be installed on client systems, meaning that they are not good solutions for applications that do not allow you to install software on the client.

type 2

The type 2 drivers are native API drivers. This means that the driver contains Java code that calls native C or C++ methods provided by the individual database vendors that perform the database access. Again, this solution requires software on the client system.

type 3

Type 3 drivers provide a client with a generic network API that is then translated into database specific access at the server level. In other words, the JDBC driver on the client uses sockets to call a middleware application on the server that translates the client requests into an API specific to the desired driver. As it turns out, this kind of driver is extremely flexible since it requires no code installed on the client and a single driver can actually provide access to multiple databases.

type 4

Using network protocols built into the database engine, type 4 drivers talk directly to the database using Java sockets. This is the most direct pure Java solution. In nearly every case, this type of driver will come only from the database vendor.

Table 4-1 lists the driver vendors that were public at the time of this book's publication. See *http://splash.javasoft.com/jdbc/jdbc.vendors.html* for a current list of JDBC vendors.

Table 4-1. A List of JDBC Driver Vendors

Vendor	Type	Supported Databases
Agave Software Design	3	Oracle, Sybase, Informix, ODBC supported databases
Asgard Software	3	Unisys A series DMSII database
Borland	4	InterBase 4.0
Caribou Lake Software	3	CA-Ingres
Center for Imaginary Environments	4	mSQL
Connect Software	4	Sybase, MS SQL Server
DataRamp	3	ODBC supported databases
IBM	2/3	IBM DB2 Version 2
IDS Software	3	Oracle, Sybase, MS SQL Server, MS Access, Informix, Watcom, ODBC supported databases
InterSoft	3	Essentia
Intersolv	2	Oracle, Sybase

Table 4-1. A List of JDBC Driver Vendors (continued)

Vendor	Type	Supported Databases
JavaSoft	1	ODBC supported databases
OpenLink	3	CA-Ingres, Postgres95, Progress, Unify
SAS	4	SAS, and via SAS/ACCESS, Oracle, Informix, Ingres, and ADABAS
SCO	3	Informix, Oracle, Ingres, Sybase, Interbase
StormCloud Development	3	ODBC supported databases
Sybase	3/4	Sybase SQL Server, SQL Anywhere, Sybase IQ, Replication Server
Symantec	3	Oracle, Sybase, MS SQL Server, MS Access, Watcom, ODBC supported databases
Visigenic	3	ODBC supported databases
WebLogic	2/3	Oracle, Sybase, MS SQL Server/ODBC supported databases

Alternatives to JDBC

Without JDBC, only disparate, proprietary database access solutions exist. These proprietary solutions force the developer to build a layer of abstraction on top of them in order to create database independent code. Only after that abstraction layer is complete can the developer move to actually writing the application. In addition, the experience you have with that abstraction layer does not translate immediately to other projects or other employers who are almost certainly using their own abstraction layers to provide access to a variety of database engines.

Of course, the ODBC specification exists to provide this universal abstraction layer for languages like C and C++ as well as popular development tools such as Delphi, PowerBuilder, and VisualBasic. Unfortunately, ODBC does not enjoy the platform independence of Java. Using the JDBC interface design, however, your server application can pick the database at runtime based on which client is connecting. The ATM front-end of the banking application, for example, could have some legacy data stored in an Oracle system that is not yet converted to the Informix system against which the rest of the application is running. You write the application without writing special access code for the legacy data. The ATM client just passes the Oracle URL when requesting the connect. Once its data has been converted to Informix, all you have to do to switch the application to the new database is tell the ATM machine about the new database URL. No new code needs to be written for the migration.

Connecting to the Database

Now I am going to dive into the details about JDBC calls and how to use them. Any JDBC application we write needs to be able to run from start to finish without ever referencing a specific JDBC implementation. Figure 4-2 shows how an application uses JDBC to talk to one or more databases without knowing any of the details concerning the driver implementation for that database. An application uses JDBC as an interface through which it passes all of its databases requests.

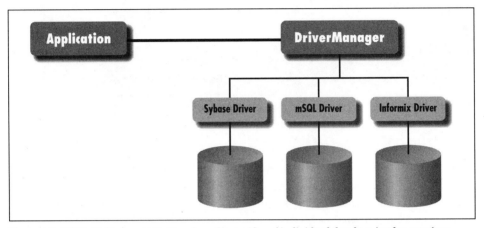

Figure 4-2. JDBC shields an application from the specifics of individual database implementations

When you write a Java database applet or application, the only driver-specific information JDBC requires from you is the database URL. You can even build your application so that it derives the URL at runtime—based on user input or applet parameters.

Using the database URL, a user name, and password, your application will first requests a `java.sql.Connection` implementation from the `DriverManager`. The `DriverManager` in turn will search through all of the known `java.sql.Driver` implementations for one that will connect with the URL you provided. If it exhausts all of the implementations without finding a match, it throws an exception back to your application.

Once a `Driver` recognizes your URL, it creates a database connection using the user name and password you specified. It then provides the `DriverManager` with a `java.sql.Connection` implementation representing that database connection. The `DriverManager` then passes that `Connection` object back to the application. In your code, the entire database connection process is handled by this one-liner:

```
Connection con = DriverManager.getConnection(url, uid, password);
```

Of course, you are probably wondering just how the JDBC `DriverManager` learns about a new driver implementation. The `DriverManager` actually keeps a list of classes that implement the `java.sql.Driver` interface. Somehow, somewhere, your application needs to load the `Driver` implementations for any potential database drivers it might require. JDBC requires a `Driver` class to register itself with the `DriverManager` when it gets loaded. The very act of loading a `Driver` class thus enters it in the `DriverManager`'s list. Your only task is thus to determine the somehow and somewhere of loading those `Driver` implementations. You have several alternatives:

Explicitly call new *to load your driver's implementation of* `Driver`
> In other words, you hard code the loading of a `Driver` implementation in your application. This alternative is the least desirable since it requires a rewrite and recompile if your database or database driver changes.

Use the jdbc.drivers *property*
> The `DriverManager` will load all classes listed in this property automatically. This alternative works well for applications with a command-line interface, but might not be so useful in GUI applications and applets. This is because you can specify properties at the command line or in environment variables. While environment variables do work for GUI applications, you cannot rely on them in Java applets.

Load the class using `Class.forName("DriverImplementationClass");`
> You can use this Java mechanism for loading classes dynamically based on a `String` with the class name. This **static** method in the `Class` class returns the Java class represented by `String` you pass. A side-effect of this behavior is that the **static** constructor in that class will be executed. JDBC requires that the **static** constructor for a `Driver` implementation load an instance of the `Driver`. As I said earlier, when you load a `Driver`, it registers itself with the `DriverManager`.

I use the third alternative almost exclusively in the examples in this book since it requires no hard-coded class names and runs well in all Java environments.

The JDBC Classes for Creating a Connection

As you can see from the process flow above, JDBC uses one class (`java.sql.DriverManager`) and two interfaces (`java.sql.Driver` and `java.sql.Connection`) for connecting to a database.

`java.sql.Driver`
> Unless you are writing your own custom JDBC implementation, you should never have to deal with this class from your application. It simply gives JDBC a launching point for database connectivity by responding to `DriverManager`

connection requests and providing information about the implementation in question.

`java.sql.DriverManager`

Unlike most other parts of JDBC, `DriverManager` is a class instead of an interface. Its main responsibility is to maintain a list of Driver implementations and present an application with one that matches a requested URL. The `Driver-Manager` provides `registerDriver()` and `deregisterDriver()` methods, which allow a Driver implementation to register itself with the `Driver-Manager` or remove itself from that list. You can get an enumeration of registered drivers through the `getDrivers()` method.

`java.sql.Connection`

The `Connection` class represents a single logical database transaction. In other words, you use the `Connection` class for sending a series of SQL statements to the database and managing the committing or aborting of those statements.

Example 4-2 puts the process of connecting to the database into a more concrete format.

Example 4-2. A Simple Database Connection

```
package example.sql;

import java.sql.Connection;
import java.sql.DriverManager;
import java.sql.SQLException;

/**
 * The SimpleConnection class is a command line application that accepts
 * the following command line:
 * java SimpleConnection DRIVER URL UID PASSWORD
 * If the URL fits the specified driver, it will then load the driver and
 * get a connection.
 */
public class SimpleConnection {
  static public void main(String args[]) {
    Connection connection;

    // Process the command line
    if( args.length != 4 ) {
      System.out.println("Syntax: java SimpleConnection " +
                         "DRIVER URL UID PASSWORD");
      return;
    }
    try { // load the driver
      Class.forName(args[0]);
```

Example 4-2. A Simple Database Connection (continued)

```
    }
    catch( Exception e ) { // problem loading driver, class not exist?
      e.printStackTrace();
      return;
    }
    try {
      connection = DriverManager.getConnection(args[1]. args[2], args[3]);
      System.out.println("Connection successful!");
      // Do whatever queries or updates you want here!!!
    }
    catch( SQLException e ) {
      e.printStackTrace();
    }
    finally {
        try {
            connection.close();
        }
        catch( SQLException e ) {
            e.printStackTrace();
        }
    }
}
```

In connecting to the database, this example catches an SQLException. This is a sort of catch-all exception for database errors. Just about any time something goes wrong between JDBC and the database, JDBC throws an SQLException. In addition to the information you commonly find in Java exceptions, SQLException also provides database specific error information, such as the SQLState value and vendor error code. JDBC SQLExceptions may be chained together so that you can find out everything that went wrong with a catastrophic database call.

Basic Database Access

Now that you are connected to the database, you can begin making updates and queries. The most basic kind of database access involves writing JDBC code where you know ahead of time whether the statements you are sending are updates (INSERT, UPDATE, or DELETE) or queries (SELECT). In the next chapter, we will discuss more complex database access that allows you to execute statements of unknown types.

Basic database access starts with the Connection object you created in the previous section. When this object first gets created, it is simply a direct link to the database. You use a Connection object to generate implementations of java.sql.Statement tied to the same database transaction. After you have used one or more Statement objects generated by your Connection, you can use it to commit or rollback the `Statement` objects associated with that `Connection`.

A `Statement` is very much what its name implies—an SQL statement. Once you get a `Statement` object from a `Connection`, you have what amounts to a blank check that you can write against the transaction represented by that `Connection`. You do not actually assign SQL to the `Statement` until you are ready to send the SQL to the database.

This is where it becomes important to know what type of SQL you are sending to the database, because JDBC uses a different method for sending queries than for sending updates. The key difference is the fact that the method for queries returns an instance of `java.sql.ResultSet` while the method for non-queries returns an integer. A `ResultSet` provides you with access to the data retrieved by a query.

Basic JDBC Database Access Classes

`java.sql.Statement`

The `Statement` class is the most basic of three JDBC classes representing SQL statements. It performs all of the basic SQL statements we have discussed so far. In general, a simple database transaction uses only one of the three statement execution methods in the `Statement` class. The first such method, `executeQuery()`, takes an SQL `String` as an argument and returns a `ResultSet` object. This method should be used for any SQL calls that expect to return data from the database. Update statements, on the other hand, are executed using the `executeUpdate()` method. This method returns the number of affected rows.

Finally, the `Statement` class provides an `execute()` method for situations in which you do not know whether the SQL being executed is a query or update. This usually happens when the application is executing dynamically created SQL statements. If the statement returns a row from the database, the method returns true. Otherwise it returns false. The application can then use the `getResultSet()` method to get the returned row.

`java.sql.ResultSet`

A `ResultSet` is a row of data returned by a database query. The class simply provides a series of methods for retrieving columns from the results of a database query. The methods for getting a column all take the form:

```
type get type(int | String)
```

where the argument represents either the column number or column name desired. A nice side effect of this design is that you can store values in the database as one type and retrieve them as a completely different type. For example, if you need a `Date` from the database as a `String`, you can get it as a `String` by calling `result_set.getString(1)` instead of calling `result_set.getDate(1)`.

Because the ResultSet class handles only a single row from the database at any given time, the class provides the `next()` method for making it reference the next row of a result set. If `next()` returns **true**, you have another row to process and any subsequent calls you make to the `ResultSet` object will be in reference to that next row. If there are no rows left, it returns **false**.

Please note that `ResultSet` objects allow only one-way navigation through rows from a query—there is no `previous()` counterpart to the `next()` method. JavaSoft is considering the addition of a `RowSet` class for Java 1.2 that will allow you to scroll through result sets in a manner similar to database cursors.

Clean Up

In the examples provided so far, you may have noticed many of the objects being closed through a `close()` method. The `Connection`, `Statement`, and `ResultSet` classes all have `close()`. A given JDBC implementation may or may not require you to close these objects before reusing. But some might, since they likely are holding precious database resources. It is therefore always a good idea to close any instance of the above objects when you are done with them. If you do manage to close a `Connection` before committing with auto-commit off, any uncommitted transactions will be lost.

Modifying the Database

In Example 4-1, we used JDBC to perform a simple SELECT query. Of course, we cannot really retrieve data from the database before we have put it there. Example 4-3 shows the simple `UpdateApp` class supplied with the Imaginary JDBC Implementation for mSQL.

Example 4-3. UpdateApp from the Imaginary JDBC Implementation for mSQL

```
import java.sql.*;

class UpdateApp {
  public static void main(String args[]) {
    Connection con;

    if( args.length != 2 ) {
      System.out.println("Syntax: <java UpdateApp [number] [string]>");
      return;
    }
```

Example 4-3. UpdateApp from the Imaginary JDBC Implementation for mSQL (continued)

```
   try {
     Class.forName("imaginary.sql.iMsqlDriver");
     String url = "jdbc:msql://athens.imaginary.com:4333/Testdb";
     con = DriverManager.getConnection(url, "borg", "");
     Statement s = con.createStatement();
     String test_id = args[0];
     String test_val = args[1];
     int update_count =
       s.executeUpdate("INSERT INTO t_test (test_id, test_val) " +
                       "VALUES(" + test_id + ", '" + test_val + "')");

     System.out.println(x + " rows inserted.");
     s.close();
   }
   catch( Exception e ) {
     e.printStackTrace();
   }
   finally {
      try { con.close(); }
      catch( SQLException e ) { e.printStackTrace(); }
   }
  }
}
```

Again, making a database call is nothing more than creating a `Statement` and passing it SQL via one of its execute methods. Unlike `executeQuery()`, however, `executeUpdate()` does not return a `ResultSet` (you should not be expecting any results). Instead, it returns the number of rows affected by the UPDATE, INSERT, or DELETE.

By default, JDBC commits each SQL statement as it is sent to the database; this is called *autocommit*. However, for more robust error handling, you can set up a `Connection` object so it issues a series of changes that have no effect on the database until you expressly send a commit. Each `Connection` is separate, and a commit on one has no effect on the statements on the other. The `Connection` class provides the `setAutoCommit()` method so you can turn autocommit off. Example 4-4 shows a simple application that turns autocommit off and commits two statements together or not at all.

Example 4-4. UpdateLogic Application That Commits Two Updates Together

```
import java.sql.*;

class UpdateLogic {
  public static void main(String args[]) {
    Connection con;
```

Example 4-4. UpdateLogic Application That Commits Two Updates Together (continued)

```
    if( args.length != 2 ) {
      System.out.println("Syntax: <java UpdateLogic [number] [string]>");
      return;
    }
    try {
      Class.forName("imaginary.sql.iMsqlDriver");
      String url = "jdbc:msql://athens.imaginary.com:4333/db_test";
      Statement s;

      con = DriverManager.getConnection(url, "borg", "");
      con.setAutoCommit(false);       // make sure auto commit is off!
      s = con.createStatement();      // create the first statement
      s.executeUpdate("INSERT INTO t_test (test_id, test_val) " +
                     "VALUES(" + args[0] + ", '" + args[1] + "')");
      s.close();                      // close the first statement
      s = con.createStatement();      // create the second statement
      s.executeUpdate("INSERT into t_test_desc (test_id, test_desc) " +
                     "VALUES(" + args[0] +
                     ", 'This describes the test.')");
      con.commit();                   // commit the two statements
      System.out.println("Insert succeeded.");
      s.close();                      // close the second statement
    }
    catch( SQLException e ) {
      if( con != null ) {
        try { con.rollback(); }       // rollback on error
        catch( SQLException e ) { }
      }
      e.printStackTrace();
    }
    finally {
      try { con.close(); }
      catch( SQLException e ) { e.printStackTrace(); }
    }
  }
}
```

The JDBC Support Classes

JDBC provides a handful of other classes and interfaces that support JDBC's core functionality. Many of them are more SQL-friendly extensions of `java.util` classes like `java.sql.Date` and `java.sql.Numeric`. Others are exception classes that get thrown by JDBC calls.

java.sql.Types

The Types class provides constants that identify SQL data types. Each constant that represents an SQL data type that is mapped to an integer is defined by the XOPEN SQL specification. You will see this class used extensively in the next chapter.

java.sql.SQLException

The SQLException class extends the general java.lang.Exception class that provides extra information about a database error. The information provided by a SQLException includes:

- The SQLState string describing the error according to the XOPEN SQLState conventions. The different values of this string are defined in the XOPEN SQL specification.

- The database-specific vendor error code. This code is usually some number that you have to look up in the obscure reference section of your database's documentation. Fortunately, the error should be sufficiently described through the Java Exception class's getMessage() method.

- A chain of exceptions leading up to this one. This is one of the niftier features of this class. Specifically, if you get several errors during the execution of a transaction, you can chain them all together in this class. This is frequently useful when you have exceptions that you want to let the user to know about, but you do not want to stop processing.

```
try {
    Connection connection = DriverManager.getConnection(url, uid,
                            pass);
}
catch( SQLException e ) {
    e.printStackTrace();
    while( (e = e.getNextException()) != null ) {
            // while more exceptions
        e.printStackTrace();
    }
}
```

java.sql.SQLWarning and java.sql.DataTruncation

Depending on the driver you are using, non-fatal errors might occur that should not halt application processing. JDBC provides an extension to the SQLException class called SQLWarning. When a JDBC object—like a ResultSet—encounters a warning situation internally, it creates an SQLWarning object and adds it to a list of warnings that it keeps. At any point, you can get the warnings for any JDBC object by repeatedly calling the `getWarnings()` method until it returns null.

The `DataTruncation` class is a special kind of warning that a JDBC implementation throws when JDBC unexpectedly truncates a data value. A `DataTruncation` object is chained as a warning on a read operation and thrown as an exception on a write.

java.sql.Date, java.sql.Time, and java.sql.Timestamp

Portable date handling among database engines can be very complex—each relational database management system (RDBMS) seems to have its own unique way of representing date information. These three classes all extend the functionality of other Java objects to provide a portable representation of their SQL counterparts. The `Date` and `Time` classes represent different levels of granularity as well as different means of expressing information already found in the `java.util.Date` class. The `java.sql.Date` class, for example, provides methods to express just the date, month, and year, while the `Time` class works in terms of hours, minutes, and seconds. And finally the `Timestamp` class takes the `java.util.Date` class down to nanosecond granularity.

java.sql.DriverPropertyInfo

I can almost guarantee that you will never use this class. It is designed for Rapid Application Development (RAD) tools like Symantec VisualCafe and Borland JBuilder. In order to provide a graphical user interface for rapid prototyping, these tools need to know what properties are required by a given JDBC implementation in order to connect to the database. Most drivers, for example, need to know the user name and password of the user connecting to the database. That and anything else the driver needs in order to connect to the database will be returned as an array of `DriverPropertyInfo` objects from the `java.sql.Driver getPropertyInfo()` method. Development tools can call this method to find out what information they should prompt the user for before connecting to the database.

5

Optimizing Database Access

The only thing that makes the device a quarter-detector rather than a slug detector or a quarter-or-slug detector is the shared intention of the device's designers, builders, owners, users. It is only in the environment or context of those users and their intentions that we can single out some of the occasions of state Q as "veridical" and others as "mistaken."

—Daniel Dennet
The Intentional Stance

In the quote above, Dennet is talking about a simple soda machine. You give it a quarter (these days, several quarters) and you get a drink. A lot of fancy mechanical stuff is in there—none of which I could begin to describe—all those parts join forces to give you a Coke whenever the machine thinks it has a quarter. An interesting problem to philosophers is that you could take this Coke machine to a country that uses *quarter-like* coins, and it will still hand you drinks. Is the soda machine mistaken when it hands you a drink? Or is it just serving a new purpose?

Applications normally interface with external systems through well-defined "black-box" interfaces very analogous to the soda machine concept. You know the name of the black box, you know what you put into it, and you know what you get out—but you may have no idea how it goes about giving you that output. Knowing what sort of inputs it expects and what sort of outputs it delivers, you can use it in new situations for which the system was not originally designed. Similarly, the designer of the black box can change the way the internals work without forcing you to change the code you have written.

You call such black boxes all the time in application code in the form of shared libraries and class libraries. It does not even matter if those libraries are written in the same language that you are using. Imagine, however, the following situation.

You are writing an application in C, and you have an operation that must be performed in Pascal. Instead of keeping that Pascal code in a separate library available to other applications, you instead choose to embed the Pascal code inside your C code. By mixing two very different programming metaphors into the same source file, you've developed an application that's both hard to program and hard to maintain.

You would never do this? So far in this book, we have been doing just that. Instead of stuffing SQL in some black box and calling it from Java by name, we have instead been formatting our SQL inside Java code and then sending that SQL to the database for interpretation. Wouldn't it be much nicer if we could just store that SQL out in the database and call it by name when we need it?

Most relational databases provide a tool for doing just that—the stored procedure. JDBC, in turn, provides advanced classes and methods that give you access to database stored procedures and more. In this chapter, we examine the JDBC stored procedure and prepared statement interfaces in addition to the more complex dynamic database access classes. Together, stored procedures and dynamic database access remove the need for hard coding information about the database you are using, so that you can create a robust set of generic database access classes that can suit your persistence needs.

Prepared SQL

Databases provide two kinds of prepared SQL: prepared statements and stored procedures. Prepared statements are much like the SQL we have been using throughout the book. They differ only in that you send the statement to the database to be interpreted before you actually use it in your application. The advantage of this approach comes when you have the same SQL being executed from inside a loop. Using the JDBC calls we have discussed so far, you send the same SQL statement to the database during each pass through the loop with only the input parameters differing. Each time the loop is executed, however, the database will re-interpret that SQL.

Your application sends a prepared statement to the database *before* you ever make a database call so that the database can interpret it and create a query plan. The query plan is the database's blueprint for executing your query. Each time you send raw SQL to the database, it builds the query plan and then executes the query according to that plan. By sending SQL as a prepared statement, you allow the database to build the query plan just once, avoiding that overhead for subsequent calls. While JDBC provides the `PreparedStatement` class for handling prepared SQL statements, it does not guarantee that the underlying database engine will take advantage of it and provide this sort of optimization.

java.sql.PreparedStatement

The `PreparedStatement` interface extends the `Statement` interface you used earlier in the book. It adds the ability to bind input parameters to your SQL call just before you execute it. By binding parameters, I mean that it allows you to associate a parameter (indicated by a placeholder like ? in the prepared statement) with an actual Java value. A situation in which you might want to use a prepared statement would be when updating a group of objects stored on the same table. For example, if you were updating many bank accounts at once, you might have a loop calling:

```
Statement statement = c.createStatement();
int i;

for(i=0; i<accounts.length; i++)
   statement.executeUpdate("UPDATE accounts " +
                        "SET balance = " + accounts[i].getBalance() +
                        "WHERE id = " + accounts[i].getId());
c.commit();
statement.close();
```

This statement creates the same query plan each time through the loop. Instead of calling this same statement over and over with different inputs, you can instead use a `PreparedStatement`:

```
PrepapredStatement statement = connection.prepareStatement(
                        "UPDATE accounts " +
                        "SET balance = ? " +
                        "WHERE id = ?");
int i;

for(i=0; i<accounts.length; i++) {
    statement.setFloat(1, accounts[i].getBalance());
    statement.setInt(2, accounts[i].getId());
    statement.execute();
}
c.commit();
statement.close();
```

With a prepared statement, you send the actual SQL to the database when you get the `PreparedStatement` object through the `prepareStatement()` method in `java.sql.Connection`. Keep in mind though, you have not yet actually executed any SQL. You execute that prepared SQL statement multiple times inside the `for()` loop, but you build the query plan only a single time.

Before each execution of the prepared statement, you tell JDBC which values to use as input for that execution of the statement. In order to bind the input parameters, `PreparedStatement` provides `setXXX()` methods (such as setFloat() and setInt()) that mirror the getXXX() methods you saw in java.sql.ResultSet. Just as the getXXX() methods read results according to the order in which you constructed your SQL, the setXXX() methods bind parameters from left to right in the order you placed them in the prepared statement. In the above example, I bind parameter 1 as a float to the account balance that I retrieve from the account object. The first ? is thus associated with parameter 1.

java.sql.CallableStatement

Prepared statements do not fit the soda machine analogy. Your SQL is still well embedded inside Java code. The java.sql.CallableStatement class provides us access to a database feature that corresponds to the soda machine analogy—the stored procedure. Stored procedures provide several advantages over embedded SQL:

- Because the procedure is precompiled in the database for most database engines, it executes much faster than dynamic SQL, which needs to be re-interpreted each time it is issued. Even if your database does not compile it before it runs, it will be precompiled for subsequent runs just like prepared statements.

- Syntax errors in the stored procedure can be caught at compile time rather than at run time.

- Java developers need to know only the name of the procedure and its inputs and outputs. The way in which the procedure is implemented—the tables it accesses, the structure of those tables, etc.—is completely unimportant.

A stored procedure is written with variables as argument place holders, which are passed when the procedure is called through column binding. Column binding is a fancy way of specifying the parameters to a stored procedure. You will see exactly how this is done in the examples ahead. A Sybase stored procedure might look like this:

```
DROP PROCEDURE sp_select_min_bal
GO


CREATE PROCEDURE sp_select_min_bal
        @balance,
AS
SELECT account_id
WHERE  balance > @balance

GO
```

The name of this stored procedure is `sp_select_min_bal`. It accepts a single argument identified by the @ sign. That single argument is the minimum balance. The stored procedure produces a result set containing all accounts with a balance greater than that minimum balance. While that stored procedure produces a result set, you can also have procedures that return output parameters. The following Oracle stored procedure calculates interest and returns the new balance:

```
CREATE OR REPLACE PROCEDURE sp_interest
(id IN INTEGER,
bal IN OUT FLOAT) IS
BEGIN
SELECT balance
INTO bal
FROM accounts
WHERE account_id = id;

bal := bal + bal * 0.03;

UPDATE accounts
SET balance = bal
WHERE account_id = id;

END;
```

In this last procedure, we have some fairly complex processing that does not (and cannot) occur in the embedded SQL we have been using so far. It actually performs two SQL statements and a calculation all in one procedure. The first part grabs the current balance, the second part takes the balance and increases it by 3%, and the third part updates the balance. In our Java application, we could use it like this:

```
try {
    CallableStatement statement;
    int i;

    statement = c.prepareCall("{call sp_interest[(?,?)]}");

    statement.registerOutParameter(2, java.sql.Types.FLOAT);
    for(i=1; i<accounts.length; i++) {
        statement.setInt(1, accounts[i].getId());
        statement.execute();
        System.out.println("New balance: " + statement.getFloat(2));
    }
    c.commit();
    statement.close();
    c.close();
}
```

The `CallableStatement` class is very similar to the `PreparedStatement` class. Using `prepareCall()` instead of `prepareStatement()`, you indicate which procedure you want to call when you initialize your `CallableStatement` object. Unfortunately, this is one place where ANSI SQL-2 simply is not enough for portability. Different database engines use different syntaxes for these calls. JDBC, however, does provide a database-independent, stored-procedure escape syntax in the form `{call procedure_name[(?, ?)]}`. For stored procedures with return values, the escape syntax is: `{? = call procedure_name[(?,?)]}`. In this escape syntax, each ? represents a place holder for either procedure inputs or return values. The JDBC driver then translates this escape syntax into the driver's own stored procedure syntax.

If your stored procedure has output parameters, you need to register their types using `registerOutParameter()` before executing the stored procedure. This tells JDBC what data type the parameter in question will be. The example above did it like this:

```
CallableStatement statement;
int i;

statement = c.prepareCall("BEGIN sp_interest(?,?); END;");
statement.registerOutParameter(2, java.sql.Types.FLOAT);
```

The processing of the loop looks just like it did for the `PreparedStatement`.

SQL Calls Contrasted with Stored Procedures

When we get to the banking application, we will need some way of creating new bank accounts and storing them in the database. If you remember back to the design we put together in Chapter 3, we will be using an `AccountPeer` whose only responsibility is to perform the database access for an account. Inserting a new account using the techniques we discussed in Chapter 4, we would have code like this:

```
public void insert(Transaction tran, Persistent p)
throws PersistenceException {
  Account account = (Account)p;
  DatabaseTransaction db = (DatabaseTransaction)tran;
  Connection conn = db.getConnection();
  // SQL for account creation
  // INSERT INTO accounts (account_id, balance, type)
  // VALUES (1, 1248.33, 'S')_
  String acct_sql = "INSERT INTO accounts " +
                    "(account_id, balance, type) " +
                    "VALUES (";
  // SQL for customer/account association
  // INSERT INTO cust_account (cust_id, account_id)
```

```
    // VALUES (1, 1)
    String ca_sql = "INSERT into cust_acct (cust_id, account_id) " +
                    "VALUES (";
    Statement statement;
    String type = p.getClass().getName();

    if( type.equals("SavingsAccount") ) {
      type ="S";
    }
    else {
      type = "C";
    }
    acct_sql = acct_sql + account.getId() + ", " +
               account.getBalance() + ", '" + type + "')";
    ca_sql = ca_sql + account.getCustomer().getId() + ", " +
               account.getId() + ")";
    try {
      statement = conn.createStatement();
      statement.executeUpdate(acct_sql);
      statement.close();
      statement = conn.createStatement();
      statement.executeUpdate(ca_sql);
      statement.close();
    }
    catch( SQLException e ) {
      throw new PersistenceException(
               "A SQLException occurred on insert: " +
               e.getMessage(), e);
    }
  }
```

Note the complex string building involved in building embedded SQL statements. Redoing it with stored procedures greatly simplifies this code:

```
  public void insert(Transaction tran, Persistent p)
  throws PersistenceException {
    String type = p.getClass().getName();

    if( type.equals("SavingsAccount") ) {
      type ="S";
    }
    else {
      type = "C";
    }
    try {
      Account account = (Account)p;
      DatabaseTransaction db = (DatabaseTransaction)tran;
      Connection conn = db.getConnection();
      CallableStatement statement;
```

```
          // insert into the accounts table
        statement = conn.prepareCall("BEGIN sp_insert account(?,?,?);
                                    END;");
        statement.setInt(1,
((Integer)account.getId().getValue()).intValue());
        statement.setFloat(2, account.getBalance());
        statement.setString(3, type);
        statement.execute();
        statement.close();
        // insert into the cust_acct table
        statement = conn.prepareCall(
                "BEGIN sp_insert_cust_acct(?,?); END;");
        statement.setInt(1,
((Integer)account.getCustomer().getId().getValue()).intValue());
        statement.setInt(2,
((Integer)account.getId().getValue()).intValue());
        statement.execute();
        conn.commit();
        statement.close();
    }
    catch( SQLException e ) {
      throw new PersistenceException(
              "A SQLException occurred on insert: " +
              e.getMessage(), e);
    }
  }
}
```

By moving to stored procedures, we have left behind any need to build SQL code inside of Java code. Instead, like a soda machine, we can throw in inputs without caring how the SQL is written to provide our outputs. Furthermore, another developer can reuse this stored procedure in a context you had not originally intended.

Database Independence Through Dynamic Access

I probably do not need to convince you that object reuse is a good thing. Who wants to rewrite old code when they could be solving new problems? You have probably noticed that, outside of the stored procedures just discussed, our JDBC code has been intimately tied to the current structure of the database we are using to solve the current problem. All of this work happens to solve today's problem, but will have to be ripped apart at our next update. If object reuse is your middle name, you must be cringing.

JDBC supports the ability to abstract away from particular programming circumstances through its dynamic database access methods and classes. For example, you might have to perform database access in which you do not know at compile time whether you will be issuing queries or updates. A very common application that faces this problem is an SQL command-line interpreter. The user issues random SQL statements; the same piece of application code must be able to handle those statements without knowing what kind of statement each one is.

Before we discussed stored procedures, we were always using the `execute-Query()` or `executeUpdate()` statements to execute SQL. That process, however, assumes that we know we are executing a query or an update. What if we wanted to write generic SQL execution as in an SQL terminal monitor?

In the discussion of stored procedures, we encountered the `execute()` method. We used it to execute stored procedures and prepared statements. It is actually a much more powerful, generic method. You can pass it any valid SQL, and it will tell you if the SQL produced a result set (in other words, if it is a query). In addition to this method, JDBC provides a pair of so-called "meta" classes that allow an application to get information about a database and about a result set.

As we use the term here, "meta" means information about your data that does not interest the end users at all, but which you need to know in order to handle the data. JDBC provides two meta-classes, `java.sql.ResultSetMetaData` and `java.sql.DatabaseMetaData`. The meta-information provided by these classes was originally included in the classes they are describing. The meta-class design, however, goes back to the fundamental JDBC goal of providing simple functionality compactly in commonly used classes and placing unusual functionality in other classes. Most people do not need such things as column data types for a result set. Placing such rarely used methods in the `ResultSet` class would serve only to complicate the introduction of new users to an otherwise simple class.

java.sql.ResultSetMetaData

As its name implies, the `ResultSetMetaData` class provides extra information about `ResultSet` objects returned from a database query. In the embedded queries we made earlier in the book, you hard-coded into your queries much of the information a ResultSetMetaData object gives you. This class provides you with answers to the following questions:

- How many columns are in the result set?
- Are column names case-sensitive?
- Can you search on a given column?
- Is NULL a valid value for a given column?
- How many characters is the maximum display size for a given column?
- What label should be used in a display header for the column?

- What is the name of a given column?

- What table did a given column come from?

- What is the data type of a given column?

If you have some generic database class that blindly receives SQL to execute from other classes, this is the sort of information you need in order to process any result sets that are produced. Take a look at the following code, for example:

```java
public Vector executeSQL(String sql) {
  Vector v = new Vector();

  try {
    Statement statement = connection.createStatement();

    if( statement.execute(sql) ) {
      ResultSet results = statement.getResultSet();
      ResultSetMetaData meta = results.getMetaData();
      int cols;

      cols = meta.getColumnCount();
      while( results.next() ) {
        Hashtable h = new Hashtable(cols);
        int i;

        for(i=0; i<cols; i++) {
          Object ob = results.getObject(i);
          h.put(meta.getColumnLabel(i), ob);
        }
        v.addElement(h);
      }
      return v;
    }
    return null;
  }
  catch( SQLException e ) {
    e.printStackTrace();
    return null;
  }
}
```

For a given `ResultSet` object, an application can call the `ResultSet`'s `getMetaData()` method in order to get its associated `ResultSetMetaData` object. You can then use this meta-data object to find out extra information about the result set and its columns. In the above example, the `execute()` method in the `Statement` class returns a `boolean` value that is true if the SQL produced a result set or false if it was a database update. Whenever the sample method executes a query producing a result set, it gets the `ResultSet` object using the `getResultSet()` method and the `ResultSetMetaData` object for that result set using the `getMetaData()` method. For each row in the result set, the example creates a `Hashtable` with column labels as keys and column values as elements. The entire set of rows is then returned as a `Vector`.

What have we gained by all of this? First, we encapsulated all database access inside a single class. In a large client/server project, handling database errors consistently becomes a huge issue, especially when the technical knowledge of the developers varies greatly. By handling all of your database access in a single class, you allow the entire application to handle database errors consistently. In order to do this, however, your database access class needs to be able to execute any possible SQL.

On a more esoteric level, dynamic database access allows vendors to create database application development tools such as the enterprise editions of Symantec's VisualCafe and Borland's JBuilder. The meta-data classes provide these tools with information about the SQL you are building with those tools, so that they can provide you with a GUI interface for database application development.

java.sql.DatabaseMetaData

As the `ResultSetMetaData` class relates to the `ResultSet` class, the `DatabaseMetaData` class relates to the `Connection` class (in spite of the naming inconsistency). The `DatabaseMetaData` class provides methods that tell you about the database for a given `Connection` object, including:

- What tables exist in the database?
- What user name is being used by this connection?
- Is this database connection read-only?
- What keywords are used by the database that are not SQL-2?
- Does the database support column aliasing?
- Are multiple result sets from a single `execute()` call supported?
- Are outer joins supported?
- What are the primary keys for a table?

The list of information provided by this class is way too long to list here, but you can check the reference section for the methods and what they do. The class is useful mostly to developer tool applications that might want to display database tables in a GUI. Most developers will rarely find a use for this class.

A Look at Our Database

We will demonstrate the power of the meta-data classes with a simple, but widely useful SQL terminal monitor application that provides a generic command-line interface to any potential database. The application should allow a user to enter SQL statements at the command line and view formatted results. We require only a single class for this example. The `main()` method creates a user input loop where the user enters commands or SQL statements. Each input is interpreted as either a command or an SQL statement. If it is interpreted as a command, the command is executed immediately. If it is not interpreted as a command, it is assumed to be part of some SQL statement and thus appended to a buffer. The application supports the following commands:

commit

Sends a commit to the database, committing any pending transactions.

go

Sends anything currently in the buffer to the database for processing as an SQL statement. The SQL is parsed through the `executeStatement()` method.

quit

Closes any database resources and exits the application.

reset

Clears the buffer without sending it to the database.

rollback

Aborts any uncommitted transactions.

show version

Displays version information on this program, the database, and the JDBC driver using the `DatabaseMetaData` interface implementation.

Example 5-1. The main() Method for an SQL Terminal Monitor Application

```
static public void main(String args[]) {
  java.io.InputStreamReader reader;
      java.io.BufferedReader input;
  Properties props = new Properties();
  Connection connection;
  boolean connected = false;
  String buffer = "", url, driver;
  int line = 1; // Mark current input line

  // Need user id and password to connect
  if( args.length < 2 ) {
    System.out.println("Syntax: <java QueryApp [user] [password]>");
    return;
```

Example 5-1. The main() Method for an SQL Terminal Monitor Application (continued)

```
      }
      props.put("user",     args[0]);
      props.put("password", args[1]);
      if( args.length > 2 ) {
        url = args[2];
      }
      else {
        url = "jdbc:msql://athens.imaginary.com:4333/db_web";
      }
      if( args.length > 3 ) {
        driver = args[3];
      }
      else {
        driver = "imaginary.sql.iMsqlDriver";
      }
      // Connect to the database
      try {
        Class.forName(driver);
        connection = DriverManager.getConnection(url, props);
      }
      catch( SQLException e ) {
        System.out.println("Failed to connect to database: " +
                           e.getMessage());
        return;
      }
      catch( ClassNotFoundException e ) {
        System.out.println("Unable to find driver class.");
        return;
      }
      System.out.println("Connected to the database.");
      connected = true;
      reader = new java.io.InputStreamReader(System.in);
      input = new java.io.BufferedReader(reader);
      // Enter into a user input loop
      while( connected ) {
        String tmp, cmd;

        // Print a prompt
        if( line == 1 ) {
          System.out.print(" > ");
        }
        else {
          System.out.print(line + "> ");
        }
        System.out.flush();
        // Get the next line of input
        try {
          tmp = input.readLine();
```

Example 5-1. The main() Method for an SQL Terminal Monitor Application (continued)

```java
    }
    catch( java.io.IOException e ) {
      return;
    }
    // Get rid of extra space in the command
    cmd = tmp.trim();
    // The user wants to commit pending transactions
    if( cmd.equals("commit") ) {
      try {
        connection.commit();
        System.out.println("Commit successful.");
      }
      catch( SQLException e ) {
        System.out.println("Error in commit: " + e.getMessage());
      }
      buffer = "";
      line = 1;
    }
    // The user wants to execute the current buffer
    else if( cmd.equals("go") ) {
      if( !buffer.equals("") ) {
        try {
          executeStatement(buffer, connection);
        }
        catch( SQLException e ) {
          System.out.println(e.getMessage());
        }
      }
      buffer = "";
      line = 1;
      continue;
    }
    // The user wants to quit
    else if( cmd.equals("quit") ) {
      connected = false;
      continue;
    }
    // The user wants to clear the current buffer
    else if( cmd.equals("reset") ) {
      buffer = "";
      line = 1;
      continue;
    }
    // The user wants to abort a pending transaction
    else if( cmd.equals("rollback") ) {
      try {
        connection.rollback();
        System.out.println("Rollback successful.");
```

Example 5-1. The main() Method for an SQL Terminal Monitor Application (continued)

```java
      }
      catch( SQLException e ) {
        System.out.println("An error occurred during rollback: " +
                            e.getMessage());
      }
      buffer = "";
      line = 1;
    }
    // The user wants version info
    else if( cmd.startsWith("show") ) {
      if( cmd.length() < 6 ) { // No argument after show
        System.out.println("show version");
      }
      else {
        DatabaseMetaData meta;

        try {
          meta = connection.getMetaData();
          cmd = cmd.substring(5, cmd.length()).trim();
          if( cmd.equals("version") ) {
            showVersion(meta);
          }
          else {
            System.out.println("show version"); // Bad arg
          }
        }
        catch( SQLException e ) {
          System.out.println("Failed to load meta data: " +
                              e.getMessage());
        }
      }
      buffer = "";
      line = 1;
    }
    // The input that is not a keyword should appended be to the buffer
    else {
      buffer = buffer + " " + tmp;
      line++;
      continue;
    }
  }
  try {
    connection.close();
  }
  catch( SQLException e ) {
    System.out.println("Error closing connection: " + e.getMessage());
  }
```

Example 5-1. The main() Method for an SQL Terminal Monitor Application (continued)

```
  System.out.println("Connection closed.");
}
```

Of course, the interesting parts of the application are in the executeState-
ment() and processResults() methods. In executeStatement(), we
blindly accept any SQL the user sends us, create a Statement, and execute it. At
that point, several things might happen:

- The SQL could have errors. If it does, display the errors to the user and
  return to the main loop for more input.

- The SQL could have been a non-query. If that is the case, let the user know
  how many rows were affected by the query.

- The SQL could have been a query. If it is, grab the result set and send it to
  processResults() for display.

Example 5-2 shows the executeStatement() method, which takes a raw SQL
string and executes it using the specified JDBC Connection object:

Example 5-2. The executeStatement() Method for the Terminal Monitor

```
static public void executeStatement(String sql, Connection connection)
throws SQLException {
  Statement statement = null;

  try {
    statement = connection.createStatement();
    if( statement.execute(sql) ) { // true means the SQL was a SELECT
      processResults(statement.getResultSet());
    }
    else { // no result sets, see how many rows were affected
      int num;

      switch(num = statement.getUpdateCount()) {
      case 0:
        System.out.println("No rows affected.");
        break;

      case 1:
        System.out.println(num + " row affected.");
        break;

      default:
        System.out.println(num + " rows affected.");
      }
    }
  }
  catch( SQLException e ) {
```

Example 5-2. The executeStatement() Method for the Terminal Monitor (continued)

```
    throw e;
  }
  finally { // close out the statement
    if( statement != null ) {
      try { statement.close(); }
      catch( SQLException e ) { }
    }
  }
}
```

In order to handle dynamic result sets, you need to use the `ResultSetMeta-Data` class. The `processResults()` method shown in Example 5-3 uses the following methods from that class:

`getColumnCount()`

   Finds out how many columns are in the result set. We need to know how many columns there are so that we do not ask for a column that does not exist or miss one that does exist.

`getColumnType()`

   Finds out the data type for each column. We need to know the data type when we retrieve it from the result set.

`getColumnLabel()`

   Gives us a display name to place at the top of each column.

`getColumnDisplaySize()`

   Tells us how wide the display of the columns should be.

Example 5-3. The processResults() Method from the Terminal Monitor Application

```
static public void processResults(ResultSet results) throws SQLException {
  try {
    ResultSetMetaData meta = results.getMetaData();
    StringBuffer bar = new StringBuffer();
    String buffer = "";
    int cols = meta.getColumnCount();
    int row_count = 0;
    int i, width = 0;

    // Prepare headers for each of the columns
    // The display should look like:
    // ------------------------------------
    // |    Column One    |   Column Two   |
    // ------------------------------------
    // |    Row 1 Value   |   Row 1 Value  |
    // ------------------------------------
```

Example 5-3. The processResults() Method from the Terminal Monitor Application (continued)

```
  // create the bar that is as long as the total of all columns
  for(i=1; i<=cols; i++) {
    width += meta.getColumnDisplaySize(i);
  }
  width += 1 + cols;
  for(i=0; i<width; i++) {
    bar.append('-');
  }
  bar.append('\n');
  buffer += bar + "|";
  // After the first bar goes the column labels
  for(i=1; i<=cols; i++) {
    StringBuffer filler = new StringBuffer();
    String label = meta.getColumnLabel(i);
    int size = meta.getColumnDisplaySize(i);
    int x;

    // If the label is long than the column is wide,
    // then we truncate the column label
    if( label.length() > size ) {
      label = label.substring(0, size);
    }
    // If the label is shorter than the column, pad it with spaces
    if( label.length() < size ) {
      int j;

      x = (size-label.length())/2;
      for(j=0; j<x; j++) {
        filler.append(' ');
      }
      label = filler + label + filler;
      if( label.length() > size ) {
        label = label.substring(0, size);
      }
      else {
        while( label.length() < size ) {
          label += " ";
        }
      }
    }
    // Add the column header to the buffer
    buffer = buffer + label + "|";
  }
  // Add the lower bar
  buffer = buffer + "\n" + bar;
  // Format each row in the result set and add it on
  while( results.next() ) {
    row_count++;
```

Example 5-3. The processResults() Method from the Terminal Monitor Application (continued)

```java
      buffer += "|";
      // Format each column of the row
      for(i=1; i<=cols; i++) {
        StringBuffer filler = new StringBuffer();
        Object value = results.getObject(i);
        int size = meta.getColumnDisplaySize(i);
        String str = value.toString();

        if( str.length() > size ) {
          str = str.substring(0, size);
        }
        if( str.length() < size ) {
          int j, x;

          x = (size-str.length())/2;
          for(j=0; j<x; j++) {
            filler.append(' ');
          }
          str = filler + str + filler;
          if( str.length() > size ) {
            str = str.substring(0, size);
          }
          else {
            while( str.length() < size ) {
              str += " ";
            }
          }
        }
        buffer = buffer + str + "|";
      }
      buffer = buffer + "\n";
    }
    // Stick a row count up at the top
    if( row_count == 0 ) {
      buffer = "No rows selected.\n" + buffer;
    }
    else if( row_count == 1 ) {
      buffer = "1 row selected.\n" + buffer + junk;
    }
    else {
      buffer = row_count + " rows selected.\n" + buffer + junk;
    }
    System.out.print(buffer);
    System.out.flush();
  }
  catch( SQLException e ) {
    throw e;
```

Example 5-3. The processResults() Method from the Terminal Monitor Application (continued)

```
  }
  finally {
    try { results.close(); }
    catch( SQLException e ) { }
  }
}
```

As a small demonstration of the workings of the `DatabaseMetaData` class, I have also added a `showVersion()` method that grabs database and driver version information from the `DatabaseMetaData` class:

```
static public void showVersion(DatabaseMetaData meta) {
  String version = "QueryApp 1.0\n";

  try {
    version += "DBMS: " + meta.getDatabaseProductName() + " " +
      meta.getDatabaseProductVersion() + "\n";
    version += "JDBC Driver: " + meta.getDriverName() + " " +
      meta.getDriverVersion();
    System.out.println(version);
  }
  catch( SQLException e ) {
    System.out.println("Failed to get version info: " +e.getMessage());
  }
}
```

6

The Application Server

Beings are, so to speak, interrogated with regard to their being. But if they are to exhibit the characteristics of their being without falsification they must for their part have become accessible in advance as they are in themselves. The question of being demands that the right access to being be gained and secured in advance with regard to what it interrogates.

—Martin Heidegger
Being and Time

In Chapter 3, we defined the objects that make up a banking application as well as a special set of objects—a persistence framework—that captures patterns we noticed in the banking application. Our design helped to answer "the question of being" surrounding these objects. We know what it is we need to build and, now that we understand JDBC, we have the tools with which to build it. In this chapter, we use this newfound JDBC knowledge to build both the persistence library and the banking application.

Persistent Objects and Their Peers

We want the persistence library to hide the persistence type (relational database, file storage, object database, etc.) from the applications we build with it. Besides sounding really cool, this technology independence is actually intuitive once you step back and think about what it is to be an account or a customer. There is nothing about the concept of a bank account that says "I save to a relational database." Instead, within the context of our application, we know that a bank account is something we wish to persist across time. How it persists is a technological detail that should not be melded into the essence of a bank account.

The core of our persistence library will contain no code specific to any data storage type. This means of course, that it does not use any of the JDBC API we learned in the previous two chapters. Figure 6-1 shows how we can structure this library so that we can write plug-in modules that support different data storage technologies without committing our applications to any particular technology.

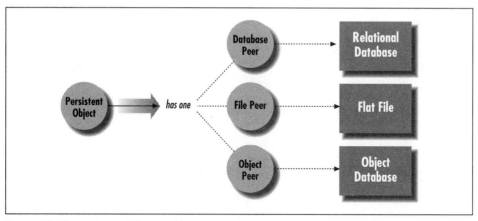

Figure 6-1. The persistence library architecture

Persistent States and Persistence Operations

What things about a bank account or a customer involve making them persistent? They save to and restore from some kind of data store. Saving is much more complex than it sounds: you could be creating a new account, updating an existing one, or deleting a closed one. Objects wanting to save an account or groups of accounts, however, should not be responsible for handling the logic that determines what kind of save a specific account requires. A persistent object should simply provide a save() method and worry how to handle that save on its own.

In order to do this, a persistent object needs to be able to track its modification state. An object can be new, unmodified, modified, or deleted. When a save is triggered, the persistent object then knows what sort of save to perform based on this modification state. Figure 6-2 provides a state transition diagram that takes us through the life cycle of a bank account.

Persistence operations may of course fail. Earlier in the book, we talked about how JDBC defaults all Connection objects to auto-committing database transactions. The persistence library will turn this feature off and allow an application to manage its own commit logic through a Transaction class. We discuss transaction logic and the Transaction class later in the chapter; however, we do need the ability in the Persistent class to know when a save has been committed or aborted.

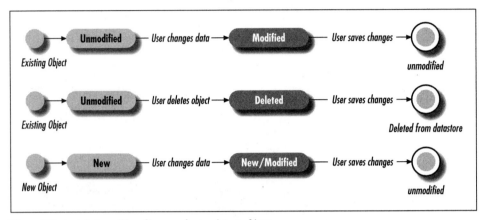

Figure 6-2. A state transition diagram for persistent objects

Take, for example, the situation in which I transfer $500 from my checking account to my savings account. Both accounts must successfully save to the database or not at all. Should one succeed and the other fail, I will end up with either $500 more or $500 less than I should have. The banking application will use the Transaction object to save both accounts and then send a commit to the JDBC Connection in the event of complete success. In the event of failure, the Transaction object instead sends a rollback to the database. This means that after save() is called in an account, the account is left in a state in which it is uncertain about whether it is part of a committed transaction or one that was rolled back because of failure. Persistent takes a couple of steps to handle this uncertainty. First, it keeps track of the fact that it is in the middle of a save. Second, it provides commit() and abort() methods to allow a Transaction to tell it whether its save() has been committed or aborted. Either way, the Persistent knows that it is done saving. After a commit, it also knows to set its state to UNMODIFIED. Figure 6-3 shows the chain of calls generated by persistence operations.

Object Locking

Another side issue we can encounter with persistent objects in a multi-user environment is that multiple people might try editing the same persistent object at the same time. In order to prevent users from overwriting each other's changes, the persistence library should provide a locking mechanism. The first client to modify an object will get a lock on that object. Other clients can view an object locked by another client, but they cannot modify it. Ideally, their user interfaces will even tell them that a particular object is locked (perhaps by changing the

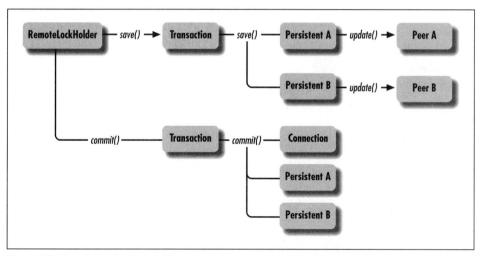

Figure 6-3. The chain of calls for all persistence operations

background color of its fields). The client owning the lock will release that lock when the client saves its changes to the data store.

This design is fraught with some peril, however. First of all, client machines have been known to crash and networks have been known to fail. In addition, users might start an edit, get a phone call, go to lunch, and leave an unsaved object locked while others are waiting to edit it. In all of these cases, we could end up with a situation in which an object is locked indefinitely.

To take care of this problem, we need to provide a way for an object to determine if a client is no longer worthy of a lock (they have taken too long) or to see if the client simply is no longer there (the machine crashed). In Figure 6-4, I provide a sketch of how a locking system that addresses these issues can work. Basically, a locked object periodically polls its lock holder to make sure the lock holder is still there.

A client window that needs to lock objects should implement an interface called `RemoteLockHolder`. Each `RemoteLockHolder` client has a `Lock` instance in the application server. Whenever a client attempts to modify a persistent object, it passes the `RemoteLockHolder` to the method that does the modification. That method compares the `Lock` object held by the `RemoteLockHolder` with any lock being held on the persistent object. If there is a lock being held and that lock is different, a `LockException` is thrown. If the locks are the same, the modification goes through. Finally, if no lock exists, the `RemoteLockHolder` gets a lock on that `Persistent` and a `LockThread` object is created to monitor that lock.

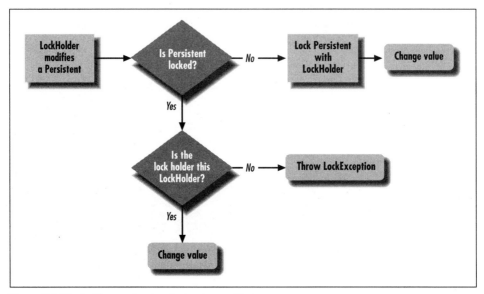

Figure 6-4. The locking mechanism for persistent objects

A LockThread is a simple class that spawns off a thread to periodically call moni-torLock() in both the Persistent and RemoteLockHolder instances. This periodic monitoring allows the LockThread to check first if there is no longer a line of communication between the client and the server. If the application server is no longer in contact with the client, the thread is stopped and the Persistent is no longer considered locked. At that point, the lock will trigger the loseLock() method in the Persistent so it has a chance to undo any changes made by the stale client. Each subclass of Persistent is therefore responsible for keeping track of the object's original data and extending lose-Lock() to restore that initial data.

Object Uniqueness

For my spouse and I to be guaranteed to see the exact same savings account instance, the application has to know when it already has that savings account loaded and when it needs to create it anew. The persistence library can provide a factory that creates all persistent objects. When a request is made for a persistent object with a certain ID, this factory should compare the ID against a master list of objects in memory. If the desired object is in that list, the class returns the object. If not, it then instantiates a new one, adds it to the list, and restores it. A pair of static methods called getPersistent() in the Persistent class handle object uniqueness. The first version provides a persistent object based on an ID, while the second one provides it based on a `Hashtable` of data taken from a data store.* Example 6-1 provides the full source for the `Persistent` class.

Example 6-1. Persistent.java, an Abstract Class for Persistent Objects

```java
/**
 * The Persistent class is an abstract base class for all
 * persistent objects.  A persistent object is any object which
 * needs to be saved to a data store.  The class does not care
 * what type of data store is used.  All code specific to a
 * particular kind of persistence is pawned off onto the
 * PersistentPeer.
 * @see imaginary.persist.PersistentPeer
 */
package imaginary.persist;

import java.util.Hashtable;
import java.util.Observable;

public abstract class Persistent extends Observable {
/************* Static persistence state values ***********/
    /**
     * The object is in the same form that is stored in the data store.
     */
    static public final int UNMODIFIED   = 1;

    /**
     * The object is brand new and has not yet been saved to the data
     * store.
     */
    static public final int NEW          = 2;

    /**
     * The object has been modified either since creation or restoring
     * from the data store.
     */
    static public final int MODIFIED     = 4;
    /**
     * The object has been deleted but is still in the data store.
     */
    static public final int DELETED      = 8;

    // The master list of objects loaded on the application server.
    // This list is a hashtable of hashtables.  For example,
    // objects.get("bank.server.Customer") returns a Hashtable of
    // all customer objects.
```

---

* Later in the chapter I will discuss the exact mechanisms used to maintain this master list as well as how objects get created with it.

Example 6-1. Persistent.java, an Abstract Class for Persistent Objects (continued)

```java
static private Hashtable objects      = new Hashtable();


/*********************** Class methods *********************/
/**
 * Given a hashtable of values taken from a data store, this class
 * method will find an existing object for that data or instantiate
 * a new one.  Once it has created that object, it will tell the
 * object to restore itself using that data.
 * @param trans the Transaction object to use for any further data
 * store access.
 * @param data the data taken from the data store for this object.
 * @param class_name the name of the class to instantiate for this
 * set of data.
 */
static public Persistent getPersistent(Transaction trans,
                   Hashtable data,
                   String class_name)
throws PersistenceException {
    Persistent p;
    Hashtable h;
    Integer i;

    // Create an instance of the specified class name
    // so that we know what the ID is.
    try {
        p = (Persistent)Class.forName(class_name).newInstance();
        p.setId(data);
    }
    catch( ClassNotFoundException e ) {
        e.printStackTrace();
        return null;
    }
    catch( InstantiationException e ) {
        e.printStackTrace();
        return null;
    }
    catch( IllegalAccessException e ) {
        e.printStackTrace();
        return null;
    }
    // Find the hashtable for this class in the objects hashtable.
    if( objects.containsKey(class_name) ) {
        h = (Hashtable)objects.get(class_name);
    }
    else {
        h = new Hashtable();
        objects.put(class_name, h);
    }
```

Example 6-1. Persistent.java, an Abstract Class for Persistent Objects (continued)

```java
        // See if this object is already in that list.
        i = new Integer(p.getId());
        if( h.containsKey(i) ) {
            return (Persistent)h.get(i);
        }
        else {
            h.put(i, p);
            // restore the new object
            p.restore(trans, data);
            return p;
        }
    }


    /**
     * Find or restore an object of the specified class based on an ID.
     * @param trans the Transaction to use for data store access.
     * @param id the ID of the object to be retrieved.
     * @param class_name the name of the class to instantiate.
     */
    static public Persistent getPersistent(Transaction trans, int id,
                        String class_name)
    throws PersistenceException {
        Integer i = new Integer(id);
        Hashtable h;

        // get the hashtable of objects for that class
        if( objects.containsKey(class_name) ) {
            h = (Hashtable)objects.get(class_name);
        }
        else {
            h = new Hashtable();
            objects.put(class_name, h);
        }
        // check if the object already exists
        if( h.containsKey(i) ) {
            return (Persistent)h.get(i);
        }
        else {
            Persistent p;

            try {
                // no instance found, load a new one
                p = (Persistent)Class.forName(class_name).newInstance();
                // set its ID
                p.setId(id);
                h.put(i, p);
                // restore it from the data store
                p.restore();
```

Example 6-1. Persistent.java, an Abstract Class for Persistent Objects (continued)

```
            }
            catch( ClassNotFoundException e ) {
                e.printStackTrace();
                return null;
            }
            catch( InstantiationException e ) {
                e.printStackTrace();
                return null;
            }
            catch( IllegalAccessException e ) {
                e.printStackTrace();
                return null;
            }
            return p;
    }
}


/****************** Instance attributes ****************/
// the object ID
private int              id              = -1;
// a Lock object is a Thread that repeatedly calls monitorLock()
private Lock             lock            = null;
// this is a bitmask of persistence states
private int              modifications = Persistent.UNMODIFIED;
// indicates a save is in progress (waiting on commit or rollback)
private boolean         saving          = false;

/********************* Constructors ******************/
/**
 * Constructor for the Persistent class.  Exports the object for
 * remote viewing.  Persistent is an abstract class, so it cannot
 * be instantiated directly.
*/
public Persistent() {
    super();
}


/****************** State check methods ***************/
/**
 * Checks to see if the object will be deleted from the data store
 * at the next save.
 * @return true if the object has been deleted.
 */
public synchronized boolean isDeleted() {
    return ((modifications & Persistent.DELETED) != 0);
}


/**
```

Example 6-1. Persistent.java, an Abstract Class for Persistent Objects (continued)

```java
 * Checks to see if a lock is being held on this object.
 * @return true if some object is locking this one
 */
public synchronized boolean isLocked() {
    return (lock != null);
}


/**
 * Checks to see if this object differs from the data store.
 * @return true if the object is new, modified, or deleted
 */
public synchronized boolean isModified() {
    // if any modifiers are present, it has been modified
    return !(modifications == Persistent.UNMODIFIED);
}


/**
 * Checks to see if this object is new and not yet in the data store.
 * This will also return false if the object has been deleted.
 * @return true if the object is new
 */
public synchronized boolean isNew() {
    if( isDeleted() ) {
        return false;
    }
    else {
        return ((modifications & Persistent.NEW) != 0);
    }
}


/**
 * Checks to see if a save operation is in progress.
 * @return true if a save operation is in progress
 */
public synchronized boolean isSaving() {
    return saving;
}


/***************** Attribute accessors ****************/
/**
 * The ID is a unique identifier for this type of object.  In real
 * situations, you probably cannot always use an int for an ID field.
 * To keep this library simple, however, we have assumed that all
 * ID's are integers.
 * @return the unique identifier for this object
 */
public synchronized int getId() {
    return id;
```

Example 6-1. Persistent.java, an Abstract Class for Persistent Objects (continued)

```
    }

    /**
     * Given a Hashtable of values taken from a data store (for example,
     * keys being column names and values being field values), a
     * persistent subclass should know which one of those fields serves
     * as the ID field for that class.  Any such class
     * should implement this method by grabbing the ID field and
     * calling setId(int).  Example:
     * <PRE>
     * public void setId(Hashtable h) {
     *     setId(((Integer)h.get("t_customer.cust_id")).intValue());
     * }
     * </PRE>
     * @param h the Hashtable of values gotten from the data store on restore
     * @see imaginary.persist.Persistent#restore
     */
    public abstract void setId(Hashtable h);

    /**
     * Sets the id field for the object.  Once an id is set, it cannot
     * be changed.
     * @param i the id to assign to the object
     */
    public synchronized void setId(int i) {
        if( id != -1 ) {
            return;
        }
        id = i;
    }

    /**
     * Modifications is a bitmask of changes which have occurred to
     * an object since it was either restored or created.
     * Unmodified objects have a Modifications value equal to
     * Persistent.UNMODIFIED.
     * @return the modification state of this object
     * @see imaginary.persist.Persistent#UNMODIFIED
     * @see imaginary.persist.Persistent#NEW
     * @see imaginary.persist.Persistent#MODIFIED
     * @see imaginary.persist.Persistent#DELETED
     */
    public synchronized int getModifications() {
        return modifications;
    }

    /**
     * Sets the modifications bitmask to NEW
```

Example 6-1. Persistent.java, an Abstract Class for Persistent Objects (continued)

```
    */
   public synchronized void setNew() {
       modifications = Persistent.NEW;
   }


   /**
    * Persistent prescribes that a subclass implement this method to
    * provide it with an instance of the peer which will perform
    * all data store access for it.
    * @return the PersistentPeer for this class
    * @see imaginary.persist.PersistentPeer
    */
   protected abstract PersistentPeer getPersistentPeer();


   /************* Transaction management methods **************/
   /**
    * When a save to the data store is aborted for any reason, this
    * method gets called in order to give the object a chance to
    * clean up.  The object should be restored to the state it was in
    * <I>immediately</I> before a save was attempted.  Within the
    * Persistent class, that simply means changing the flag indicating
    * a save is in progress.  Of course, objects extending this class
    * may or may not have their own cleanup to do.
    */
   protected synchronized void abort() throws PersistenceException {
       if( !isSaving() ) { // If object is not saving, it needs no abort
           return;
       }
       saving = false; // stop it from saving
       // keep the lock in place
   }


   /**
    * When one or more saves have been sent to the data
    * store successfully, they are committed.  This method
    * allows an object to know the pending save was successful
    * and release any locks.
    */
   protected synchronized void commit() throws PersistenceException {
       Transaction t;

       // If the object is not being saved, commit not needed
       if( !isSaving() ) {
           return;
       }
       if( !isLocked() ) {
           throw new PersistenceException(
                   "Attempt to commit an unlocked " +
```

Example 6-1. Persistent.java, an Abstract Class for Persistent Objects (continued)

```
                    "object.");
    }
    // end saving
    saving = false;
    // release lock
    lock.releaseLock(this);
    lock = null;
    // reset modification state
    if( isDeleted() ) {
        modifications = Persistent.DELETED;
    }
    else {
        modifications = Persistent.UNMODIFIED;
    }
}


/******************** Persistence operations ****************/
/**
 * This method flags the object for deletion.
 * @param h the client make the modification to this object
 * @exception imaginary.persist.LockException Attempt to delete locked
 * object by a client not holding the lock
 */
public synchronized void remove(RemoteLockHolder h)
                                throws LockException {
    // Check for a lock
    if( isLocked() ) {
        if( h.hashCode() != lock.getHolder().hashCode() ) {
            throw new LockException("Illegal attempt to delete object " +
                                    "without a lock.");
        }
    }
    // Create the lock if it does not exist
    if( !isLocked() ) {
        lock = Lock.createLock(h, this);
    }
    // Mark the object deleted
    modifications |= Persistent.DELETED;
    setChanged();
}


/**
 * This version of restore() is called for a one-off restore.  In
 * other words, you know the object ID and you want to restore just
 * this object.
 * @exception imaginary.persist.PersistenceException An error occurred
 * accessing the data store.
 */
```

Example 6-1. Persistent.java, an Abstract Class for Persistent Objects (continued)

```
protected synchronized void restore() throws PersistenceException {
    Transaction t = Transaction.getTransaction();

    t.restore(this);
}


/**
 * Given a set of query data, restore this object.
 * @param data the query data to use to restore this object
 * @exception imaginary.persist.PersistenceException An error occurred
 * accessing the data store.
 */
protected final synchronized void restore(Hashtable data)
throws PersistenceException {
    Transaction t = Transaction.getTransaction();

    t.restore(this, data);
}


/**
 * Restore this object using only its ID for the query.
 * @param t the Transaction to use to access the data store
 * @exception imaginary.persist.PersistenceException An error occurred
 * accessing the data store.
 */
public void restore(Transaction t) throws PersistenceException {
    getPersistentPeer().restore(this, t);
}


/**
 * This object's peer will go to the data store and grab all of the
 * attributes for this object.  Once it has those values, it will
 * shove them into a Hashtable and pass them to this method.
 * Objects extending the Persistent class should therefore implement
 * this method so that it takes the values out of the Hashtable and
 * assigns them to the appropriate object attributes.
 * @param t the Transaction used for the restore
 * @param data the Hashtable of object data
 * @exception imaginary.persist.PersistenceException An error occurred
 * access the data store.
 */
public abstract void restore(Transaction t, Hashtable data)
throws PersistenceException;


/**
 * This method flags the object as saving and then tells its
 * peer to perform the actual save.
 * @exception imaginary.persist.PersistenceException An error occurred
```

Example 6-1. Persistent.java, an Abstract Class for Persistent Objects (continued)

```
 * access the data store
 */
protected synchronized void save() throws PersistenceException {
    PersistentPeer peer;

    if( !isLocked() ) {
        throw new PersistenceException(
                "Attempt to save an unlocked: " +
                "object.");
    }
    peer = getPersistentPeer();
    // flag the object as saving
    saving = true;
    // determine what sort of operation is required and tell the
    // peer to do it
    if( isDeleted() ) {
        peer.remove(this, lock.getTransaction());
    }
    else if( isNew() ) {
        peer.insert(this, lock.getTransaction());
    }
    else {
        peer.update(this, lock.getTransaction());
    }
}


/****************** Locking operations ****************/
/**
 * For any number of reasons, a client holding a lock might
 * unexpectedly lose that lock.  The most common reason is simply
 * a network failure between client and server.  In that event,
 * we want to release the lock and restore the object to its
 * unmodified state.
 */
protected synchronized void loseLock() {
    lock = null;
    modifications = Persistent.UNMODIFIED;
}


/**
 * The lock has a thread that simply triggers this method
 * every now and then.  If the criteria for maintaining a lock are
 * still in force, then everything is ok.  Otherwise, a LockException
 * is thrown.  The only criteria for this lock is that the
 * client holding the lock is still accessible.  You could add
 * timeouts or whatever you like.
 * @param l the lock being tested
 * @exception imaginary.persist.LockException The lock should be lost
```

Example 6-1. Persistent.java, an Abstract Class for Persistent Objects (continued)

```
    */
    protected synchronized void monitorLock() throws LockException {
        // If we cared, we might add a "last touched" check in here
        // to have the lock timeout.
        // If so, we would throw a LockException.

        // a lock is monitored because the object has been modified
        // therefore notify any observers of those changes
        notifyObservers();
    }

    /**
     * Whenever an attribute in this object changes from its initial state,
     * this method should be called in order to change the object's state.
     * If an attempt is made to modify a locked by object a
     * RemoteLockHolder that does not hold the lock,
     * then a LockException gets thrown.
     * @param h the client making the modifications
     * @exception imaginary.persist.LockException Attempt to modify locked
     * object by a Transaction not holding the lock.
     */
    protected synchronized void modify(RemoteLockHolder h)
    throws LockException {
        // Someone is doing something they should not!
        if( isLocked() ) {
            // comparing hash codes to support equality for RMI in
            // Chapter 8
            if( h.hashCode() != lock.getHolder().hashCode() ) {
                throw new LockException("Illegal attempt to modify " +
                                        "object without a lock.");
            }
        }
        // First modification!
        if( !isLocked() ) {
            lock = Lock.createLock(h, this);
        }
        // Add Persistent.MODIFIED to the bitmask
        modifications |= Persistent.MODIFIED;
        setChanged();
    }
}
```

Object Identification

In any well-designed, object-oriented system, an object represents a unique entity. In a database, however, a unique entity is most often identified as a row in which one or more columns have a value unlike any other row. This field or set of fields is called the key. The persistence library uses the key from the database to map rows into Java objects. It specifically checks the key from a newly retrieved row and compares it against the getId() value for existing objects. In banks, the bank account number serves as the key for bank accounts. The persistence library borrows these database keys to store persistent objects in the master list held by the Persistent class. The reason for this list may appear a little murky. In simple terms, we need to keep a list of all the objects we have restored from the database so that when a request comes to restore that object again, we have it readily available.

Java provides us with two types of dynamically growable lists: hashtables and vectors. A vector (java.util.Vector) is like a more dynamic array type. You access its members by index number. This means that checking for the existence of a certain element in the vector involves walking the entire list. A hashtable (java.util.Hashtable), on the other hand, allows you to store an object in a list associated with any arbitrary object type that will uniquely identify the object. Among other things, it makes for a quicker check to see if an object exists in the list. For efficiency, I therefore chose to store these objects in a Hashtable.

The downside to java.util.Hashtable is that each key used to identify the object in the list must have a hash code returned by the hashCode() method in java.lang.Object that the Hashtable uses for storing the object. All Java objects have default hash codes. The default hash codes, however, have a major drawback: no two objects of the same class have the same hash code. The String and Integer classes avoid this problem by overriding the default Java hash-Code() method to ensure that equivalent strings and integers have the same hash code value. If you wanted your own ID class—say one that uses a last name and creation date together as the ID—and you wanted to make sure that equivalent IDs have identical hash codes, you would have to write your own hashing algorithm. This is not an endeavor you should undertake willingly. For this reason, I have simply forced all persistent objects to have int IDs. That also means that the database tables must have single column int keys. A robust persistence library would have to do much better.

Persistent Subclasses

Persistent is an abstract class. It leaves several methods to be defined by its subclasses based on what it cannot know itself. It cannot know implementation or class-specific details. For example, it cannot know that the ID field for a bank account is account_id. It cannot know that for this application a database is being used for data storage. And it cannot know how to associate data from the data store with attributes in a Customer.

In particular, `Persistent` prescribes the following three methods for its subclasses:

`void setId(Hashtable)`

> During a restore, the `PersistentFactory` (the object that maintains the master list of persistent objects) requires an object to pull its ID out of a `Hashtable` of values retrieved from the database. `PersistentFactory` calls `setId()` with that `Hashtable` to give the persistent object an opportunity to find the value representing the ID and call `setId(int)` using that value.

`PersistentPeer getPersistentPeer()`

> Throughout `Persistent`, a `PersistentPeer` (which we discuss in the next section) is used to perform functions specific to the type of data store. Subclasses are responsible for specifying exactly which object to use as a `PersistentPeer`. Conceivably, you could specify on the command line which peers to use for different persistent objects. This way you could dynamically switch between different kinds of persistence. As you will see later in the chapter, however, we are just creating an instance of a `PersistentPeer` subclass for each `Persistent` subclass and returning that instance.

`void restore(Transaction, Hashtable)`

> Your peer goes to the data store and gets all your values for you. You need to take those values and give them meaning. An implementation of this method simply takes the values from the `Hashtable` and assigns them to specific object attributes. The reason that `restore()` requires an implementation is that you might be like me and want to keep your attributes `private`. While the peer can handle saves by getting the attributes through accessor methods, you need direct access to the attributes to handle a restore. The `restore()` method therefore handles that direct access.

You will see how a persistent object implements these methods later when we go over the `Account` and `Customer` classes from the banking application.

Persistent's Peers

The most complex concept in the persistent object code is the use of the peer pattern for save and restore operations. Peers allow us to make accounts and customers persistent without saying how they are persistent. The actual peers, which we can assign at runtime, define how an object is persistent. As the persistence library object model showed, we can have database peers for database persistence and file peers for file persistence. Example 6-2 shows the Persis-tentPeer interface.

Example 6-2. The PersistentPeer Interface

```
package imaginary.persist;

public interface PersistentPeer {
    public abstract void insert(Persistent p, Transaction t)
    throws PersistenceException;

    public abstract void remove(Persistent p, Transaction t)
    throws PersistenceException;

    public abstract void restore(Persistent p, Transaction t)
    throws PersistenceException;

    public abstract void update(Persistent p, Transaction t)
    throws PersistenceException;
}
```

This interface for peers is simple. They must define ways for inserting, removing, restoring, and deleting persistent objects. Later in the chapter, I show how this class is implemented for database access.

Transaction Management

It is a rare situation when you handle one object at a time. In the banking application, for example, we want to show a customer all accounts belonging to that customer. We therefore need a way to retrieve all those accounts. In addition, we need to be able to save a transfer of money from one account to the next as a single operation. Transaction management allows us to perform persistence operations on multiple objects as a single unit.

In order to handle transaction management cleanly, I am introducing a lot of classes that come at you all at once. From a conceptual point of view, you have a client who wants to make changes to one or more accounts and commit those changes as a single transaction. From the time the first edit is made until the time the changes are successfully committed, the client wants to know that it has exclusive rights to make changes to the account. No one else should be able to come in and blow away those changes.

From this point of view, the client is a lock holder who holds a lock associated with a transaction. The lock uses that transaction to make changes to accounts. When an object is newly modified in the name of a particular lock holder, that lock holder's lock creates a thread to periodically check with the object to see if the lock is still valid and allow that object to notify others of changes.* Finally, when the lock holder is done, it tells the lock to save all objects it has modified. If all of the saves are successful, the transaction commits the changes to the data store and notifies the objects that their save was successful; otherwise, the transaction rolls back the changes and sends an abort to the affected objects. Figure 6-5 describes this process graphically.

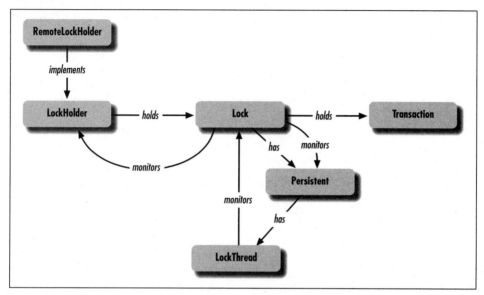

Figure 6-5. The transaction management classes of the persistence library

Transactions

The Transaction class is the main object behind this transaction management scheme. It is owned by a lock associated with a client object implementing the RemoteLockHolder interface. The RemoteLockHolder interface looks like this:

```
package imaginary.persist;

public interface RemoteLockHolder {
    public abstract void monitorLock(Persistent p);

    public abstract void setLock(Lock lock);
}
```

---

* We will implement the notification of other objects in the next chapter.

The client RemoteLockHolder will pass itself to all Persistent objects when changes are made. If you remember back to the Persistent class in Example 6-1, each time modify() is called, it creates a lock if none exists. The Transaction object for that lock keeps track of all the Persistent objects that a client locks. When the user performs some action to launch the saving of these objects (like clicking a save button), the RemoteLockHolder can call the save() method in the Lock to trigger its Transaction to handle everything associated with a save. Example 6-3 provides the source code for the Transaction class.

Example 6-3. Transaction.java

```
/**
 * The Transaction class is an abstract class implemented by different
 * persistence packages for managing persistence operations on groups
 * of objects.  A Transaction gets created based on a data store URL
 * that tells the Transaction object what type of data store it is dealing
 * with, as well as where that data store is.
 */
package imaginary.persist;

import java.util.Properties;
import java.util.Vector;

public abstract class Transaction {
    static public Properties properties = null;
    static public String     url        = null;

    static public Transaction getTransaction() throws PersistenceException
    {
        return new DatabaseTransaction(url, properties);
    }

    /********************** Instance attributes ******************/
    /**
     * The list of objects modified by this Transaction.
     */
    private Vector objects = new Vector();


    /************************ Constructors ********************/
    /**
     * Creates a new transaction object.
     */
    public Transaction() {
        super();
    }
```

Example 6-3. Transaction.java (continued)

```
/***************** Attribute accessors ******************/
/**
 * Adds a Persistent as part of the Transaction
 * @param p the Persistent to be part of the Transaction
 */
synchronized void addPersistent(Persistent p) {
    if( !objects.contains(p) ) {
        objects.addElement(p);
    }
}


/**
 * @return an array of Persistent objects associated with this
 * Transaction
 */
synchronized Persistent[] getPersistents() {
    Persistent[] obs = new Persistent[objects.size()];

    objects.copyInto(obs);
    return obs;
}


/**
 * Removes a Persistent from the Transaction
 * @param p the Persistent to be removed
 */
synchronized void removePersistent(Persistent p) {
    if( objects.contains(p) ) {
        objects.removeElement(p);
    }
}


/************** Persistence operations ***************/
/**
 * Aborts any persistence operations in process and allows
 * persistent objects which have already done their operation
 * to take it back.
 */
public void abort() {
    Persistent[] obs = getPersistents();

    for(int i=0; i<obs.length; i++) {
        try {
            if( obs[i].isSaving() ) {
                obs[i].abort();
            }
        }
        catch( PersistenceException e ) {
```

Example 6-3. Transaction.java (continued)

```
                e.printStackTrace();
        }
    }
}


/**
 * This method should be extended in data store specific
 * transaction objects for sending a commit to the data store.
 * Within the Transaction class, it lets all locked objects know
 * that any data store commit was successful.
 * @exception imaginary.persist.PersistenceException An error occurred
 * trying to commit.
 */
public void commit() throws PersistenceException {
    Persistent[] obs = getPersistents();

    for(int i=0; i<obs.length; i++) {
      if( obs[i].isSaving() ) {
          obs[i].commit();
      }
    }
    // commit done, prepare for new set of modifications
    objects = new Vector();
}


/**
 * Calls for the restoration of a particular object using this
 * Transaction.
 * @param p the object to restore using this Transaction
 */
public void restore(Persistent p) throws PersistenceException {
    p.restore(this);
}


/**
 * Calls for the restoration of the specified Persistent using
 * a hashtable of query parameters.
 * @param p the Persistent to restore
 * @param data the query parameters
 */
public void restore(Persistent p, Hashtable data)
throws PersistenceException {
    p.restore(this, data);
}


/**
 * Calls for the restoration of the specified PersistentSet
 * using a hashtable of query parameters.
```

Example 6-3. Transaction.java (continued)

```
    * @parameter set a set to be restored
    * @param data the query parameters for the restore
    */
   public void restore(PersistentSet set, Hashtable data)
   throws PersistenceException {
       set.restore(this, data);
   }


   /**
    * This method goes through and triggers a save on all locked objects.
    * If the saves are all successful, then a commit() is triggered.  If
    * any one of the saves fails, however, then an abort() is triggered.
    * @exception imaginary.persist.PersistenceException An error
    * triggering an abort occurred.
    */
   public void save() throws PersistenceException {
       Persistent[] obs = getPersistents();

       for(int i=0; i<obs.length; i++) {
           try {
               if( obs[i].isModified() ) { // only save modified objects
                   obs[i].save();
               }
           }
           catch( PersistenceException e ) {
               abort(); // abort on error
               throw e;
           }
       }
       try {
           commit(); // commit on success
       }
       catch( PersistenceException e ) {
           abort(); // abort if the commit failed
           throw e;
       }
   }
}
```

Object Sets

In an application, you probably will create multiple views of the same objects. One window, for example, could show all of the accounts for a particular user. Another administrative window, however, might show all accounts with less than $100. If you opened both windows at the same time, you could end up with two different views that contain one or more of the same object.

The persistence library uses the concept of a set to handle groups of objects of the same type. The `PersistentSet` class is responsible for restoring a group of `Persistent` objects of the same set using the `Persistent` class method `getPersistent()` and then keeping track of those objects. If you remember back to Chapter 3, I stated that a factory was a special pattern that lets you handle the creation of objects in a single place. We need to handle the creation of `Persistent` instances in a single place because we do not want to create multiple instances of the same object. In other words, when you log in and two seconds later your spouse logs in, your spouse's client should be referring to the exact same account object as you, not another instance of that account object. The `Persistent` holds a master `Hashtable` of persistent objects. When a request is made by a `PersistentSet` to create a new object based on a row from a database, it first checks to see if the object is already in memory. If it is, it simply returns that object. If not, it creates an instance of that class and calls `restore()` in the object. Figure 6-6 shows the process flow of restoring one or more objects from the data store based on search criteria.

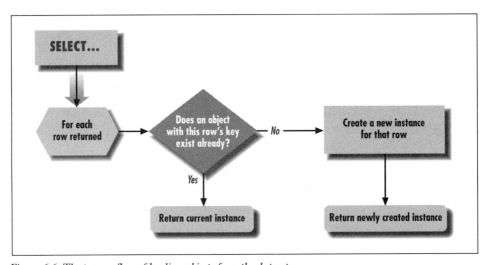

Figure 6-6. The process flow of loading objects from the data store

Example 6-4 shows the code for a `PersistentSet`.

Example 6-4. PersistentSet.java

```
/**
 * A PersistentSet represents a group of Persistent objects
 * based on certain query criteria.
 */
package imaginary.persist;
```

Example 6-4. PersistentSet.java (continued)

```java
import java.util.Hashtable;
import java.util.Observable;
import java.util.Vector;

public abstract class PersistentSet extends java.util.Observable
    /****************** Instance attributes ***************/
    // objects in the set
    private Vector        objects     = new Vector();

    /******************** Constructors *******************/
    /**
     * Creates a new PersistentSet.
     */
    public PersistentSet() {
        super();
    }


    /*************** Attribute accessors ****************/
    /**
     * Called by its peer to add a restored Persistent to the set.
     * @param p the Persistent to be added to the set
     */
    public synchronized void addPersistent(Persistent p) {
        if( !objects.contains(p) ) {
            objects.addElement(p);
        }
    }


    /**
     * Allows external objects to get a list of the Persistent objects
     * in this set.
     * @return the Persistent objects in the set
     */
    public synchronized Persistent[] getPersistents() {
        Persistent[] persistents = new Persistent[objects.size()];

        objects.copyInto(persistents);
        return persistents;
    }


    /**
     * Subclasses must implement this method in order to tell
     * this class what to use for a PersistentSetPeer.
     * @return the peer for this set
     */
    protected abstract PersistentSetPeer getPersistentSetPeer();

    /**************** Persistence operations ***************/
```

Example 6-4. PersistentSet.java (continued)

```java
    /**
     * Loads the set without any query criteria.  In other words,
     * it loads all objects of a given type.
     * @exception imaginary.persist.PersistenceException An error occurred
     * in accessing the database.
     */
    public synchronized void restore() throws PersistenceException {
        Transaction t = Transaction.getTransaction();

        t.restore(this, null);
    }


    /**
     * Loads a set of persistent objects based on query criteria listed in
     * the Hashtable values.
     * @param h the values for filtering the objects of a specific type
     * @exception imaginary.persist.PersistenceException An error occurred
     * in accessing the database.
     */
    public synchronized void restore(Hashtable h)
                            throws PersistenceException {
        Transaction t = Transaction.getTransaction();

        t.restore(this, h);
    }


    /**
     * Loads a set of persistent objects based on query criteria listed in
     * the Hashtable values.
     * @param trans the Transaction object to use for the restore
     * @param data the values for filtering the objects of a specific type
     * @exception imaginary.persist.PersistenceException An error occurred
     * in accessing the database.
     */
    public synchronized void restore(Transaction trans, Hashtable data)
    throws PersistenceException {
        getPersistentSetPeer().restore(this, trans, data);
    }
}
```

Like the `Persistent` class, this class uses a peer to perform data store specific operations. Unlike the `Persistent` class's peer, this peer is concerned only with restore operations. Example 6-5 shows the `PersistentSetPeer` interface.

Example 6-5. PersistentSetPeer.java

```java
/**
 * The PersistentSetPeer interface prescribes methods for data store
```

Example 6-5. PersistentSetPeer.java (continued)

```
 * specific operations.
 */
package imaginary.persist;

import java.util.Hashtable;

public interface PersistentSetPeer {
    public abstract void restore(PersistentSet set, Transaction t)
    throws PersistenceException;

    public abstract void restore(PersistentSet set, Transaction t,
                                 Hashtable h)
    throws PersistenceException;
}
```

Other than the exception classes, I have omitted only one of the general persistence classes. The Lock class is simply a class that keeps track of the relationship between RemoteLockHolder objects and the Persistent objects they lock. You can find the source code in the reference section as well as online with the rest of this book's source code.

Database Persistence

Now that we have a general foundation for object persistence, we can use these classes to create a database persistence package. The general library clearly set aside the peer classes and the Transaction class as the places where data-store-specific persistence operations should occur. In order to create a database persistence library, we thus need to create database-specific extensions of these three classes.

Here we get the chance to put our JDBC skills to use. In the first extension, the DatabaseTransaction class, we essentially use the Transaction as a java.sql.Connection wrapper. As such, it only triggers the aborts and commits in the JDBC Connection object. It does absolutely nothing else. Example 6-6 is the DatabaseTransaction class.

Example 6-6. DatabaseTransaction.java

```
/**
 * The DatabaseTransaction class basically serves as a wrapper
 * around the JDBC Connection class.  It allows peers access to
 * the JDBC Connection in addition to triggering commits and rollbacks
 * as needed by the persistence package.
 */
package imaginary.persist;
```

Example 6-6. DatabaseTransaction.java (continued)

```java
import java.sql.Connection;
import java.sql.DriverManager;
import java.sql.SQLException;
import java.util.Hashtable;
import java.util.Properties;

public class DatabaseTransaction extends Transaction {
    private Connection connection = null;
    private Properties properties = null;
    private String       url       = null;


    /******************** Constructors ********************/
    /**
     * Creates a DatabaseTransaction using the specified URL and
     * properties.
     * @param holder the remote lock holder
     * @param url the JDBC URL for this DatabaseTransaction
     * @param p the properties, generally containing user name and password
     * @exception imaginary.persist.PersistenceException An error occurred
     * finding a JDBC driver for the URL
     */
    public DatabaseTransaction(String u, Properties p)
    throws PersistenceException {
        super();
        url = u;
        properties = p;
    }


    /*************** Attribute Accessors ******************/
    /**
     * @return the JDBC Connection for this DatabaseTransaction
     */
    public synchronized Connection getConnection() {
        return connection;
    }


    /************* Persistence operations ****************/
    /**
     * Upon a successful JDBC rollback, this will trigger the
     * inherited abort() method.
     * @see imaginary.persist.Transaction#abort
     */
    public synchronized void abort() {
        try {
            connection.rollback();
            super.abort();
        }
```

Example 6-6. DatabaseTransaction.java (continued)

```java
        catch( SQLException e ) {
        }
    }

    /**
     * Upon a successful JDBC commit, this will call the inherited
     * commit in order to let all committed objects know the commit
     * was successful.
     * @exception imaginary.persist.PersistenceException An error occurred
     * attempting to commit the transaction
     */
    public synchronized void commit() throws PersistenceException {
        try {
            connection.commit();
            super.commit();
        }
        catch( SQLException e ) {
            abort();
            throw new PersistenceException(e);
        }
    }

    /**
     * Restores a specific persistent object.
     * @param p the Persistent to restore
     */
    public synchronized void restore(Persistent p)
    throws PersistenceException {
        if( connection == null ) {
            try {
                connection = DriverManager.getConnection(url, properties);
                // comment out setAutoCommit() for mSQL
                // which does not handle transaction logic
                // connection.setAutoCommit(false);
            }
            catch( SQLException e ) {
                throw new PersistenceException(e);
            }
        }
        try {
            super.restore(p);
        }
        finally {
            try {
                connection.close();
            }
            catch( SQLException e ) {
                e.printStackTrace();
```

Example 6-6. DatabaseTransaction.java (continued)

```java
            }
            connection = null;
        }
    }

    /**
     * Restores a persistent with the specified data.
     * @param p the persistent object to restore
     * @param data the data to use for restoring the object
     */
    public synchronized void restore(Persistent p, Hashtable data)
    throws PersistenceException {
        if( connection == null ) {
            try {
                connection = DriverManager.getConnection(url, properties);
            }
            catch( SQLException e ) {
                throw new PersistenceException(e);
            }
        }
        try {
            super.restore(p, data);
        }
        finally {
            try {
                connection.close();
            }
            catch( SQLException e ) {
                e.printStackTrace();
            }
            connection = null;
        }
    }

    /**
     * Restores a PersistentSet based on the specified query criteria.
     * @param set the set to be restored
     * @param data the query parameter to use for the restore
     */
    public synchronized void restore(PersistentSet set, Hashtable data)
    throws PersistenceException {
        if( connection == null ) {
            try {
                connection = DriverManager.getConnection(url, properties);
                // connection.setAutoCommit(false);
            }
            catch( SQLException e ) {
                throw new PersistenceException(e);
```

Example 6-6. DatabaseTransaction.java (continued)

```
            }
        }
        try {
            super.restore(set, data);
        }
        finally {
            try {
                connection.close();
            }
            catch( SQLException e ) {
                e.printStackTrace();
            }
            connection = null;
        }
    }


    /**
     * Saves all of the objects associated with this object using
     * database persistence.
     */
    public synchronized void save() throws PersistenceException {
        if( connection == null ) {
            try {
                connection = DriverManager.getConnection(url, properties);
                // connection.setAutoCommit(false);
            }
            catch( SQLException e ) {
                throw new PersistenceException(e);
            }
        }
        try {
            super.save();
        }
        finally {
            try {
                if( connection != null ) {
                    connection.close();
                }
            }
            catch( SQLException e ) {
                e.printStackTrace();
            }
            connection = null;
        }
    }
}
```

Both peers require the `Connection` object from the `DatabaseTransaction` class in order to execute their SQL statements. The peers themselves are the very soul of database access for the database portion of the persistence library. The `DatabasePeer` handles saves and restores for individual objects from the database. The `DatabaseSetPeer` class, on the other hand, handles restores for groups of persistent objects from the database. In both cases, all database access is done through JDBC. Example 6-7 shows the code for the `DatabasePeer`.

Example 6-7. DatabasePeer.java

```
/**
 * The DatabasePeer class implements the persistence methods
 * from PersistentPeer and performs the actual database access
 * for individual persistent objects.  Of course, at this level
 * it is impossible to know everything about the application in
 * order to isolate database access completely. Applications such
 * as ours that require database persistence should extend this
 * class and implement the abstract methods that allow an application
 * to formulate the SQL.
 */
package imaginary.persist;

import java.sql.Connection;
import java.sql.ResultSet;
import java.sql.ResultSetMetaData;
import java.sql.SQLException;
import java.sql.Statement;
import java.util.Hashtable;

public abstract class DatabasePeer implements PersistentPeer {
    /**
     * Subclasses must implement this method to build an INSERT
     * statement for the specified persistent object.
     * @param p the Persistent that is being inserted into the database
     * @return the SQL string to be sent to the database
     */
    protected abstract String getInsertSql(Persistent p);

    /**
     * Subclasses must implement this method to build a DELETE
     * statement for the specified persistent object.
     * @param p the Persistent that is being deleted from the database
     * @return the SQL DELETE statement
     */
    protected abstract String getRemoveSql(Persistent p);

    /**
     * Subclasses must implement this method to build a SELECT
     * statement that will restore only the named persistent object.
```

Example 6-7. DatabasePeer.java (continued)

```
 * At the time it gets passed to this method, the persistent
 * object has only its ID set.  All other values are awaiting
 * a restore operation.
 * @param p the Persistent that is being restored from the database
 * @return the SQL SELECT statement
 */
protected abstract String getRestoreSql(Persistent p);

/**
 * Subclasses must implement this method to build an UPDATE
 * statement that will update the specified persistent object.
 * @param p the Persistent object to be updated
 * @return the SQL UPDATE statement
 */
protected abstract String getUpdateSql(Persistent p);

/**
 * This method implements the insert persistence operation
 * as prescribed by the PersistentPeer interface.  It asks
 * its subclasses for the proper SQL and then triggers
 * a save using that SQL statement.
 * @param p the persistent object to be inserted
 * @param t the DatabaseTransaction to use for that insert
 * @exception imaginary.persist.PersistenceException An error occurred
 * in saving the object to the database.
 */
public void insert(Persistent p, Transaction t)
throws PersistenceException {
    save((DatabaseTransaction)t, getInsertSql(p));
}

/**
 * This method implements the remove persistence operation
 * as prescribed by the PersistentPeer interface.  It asks
 * its subclasses for the proper SQL and then triggers
 * a save using that SQL statement.
 * @param p the persistent object to be removed
 * @param t the DatabaseTransaction to use for that removal
 * @exception imaginary.persist.PersistenceException An error occurred
 * in removing the object from the database.
 */
public void remove(Persistent p, Transaction t)
throws PersistenceException {
    save((DatabaseTransaction)t, getRemoveSql(p));
}

/**
 * This method implements the restore persistence operation
```

Example 6-7. DatabasePeer.java (continued)

```
 * as prescribed by the PersistentPeer interface.  It asks
 * its subclasses for the proper SQL and then triggers
 * a save using that SQL statement.
 * @param p the persistent object to be restored
 * @param t the DatabaseTransaction to use for restoring the object
 * @exception imaginary.persist.PersistenceException An error occurred
 * in restoring the object from the database.
 */
public void restore(Persistent p, Transaction trans)
throws PersistenceException {
    String sql = getRestoreSql(p); // get the restore SQL
    Connection connection = null;
    Statement statement = null;
    ResultSet results = null;
    ResultSetMetaData meta = null;

    try {
        Hashtable h = new Hashtable(); // store the values here

        // Get the connection from the DatabaseTransaction
        connection = ((DatabaseTransaction)trans).getConnection();
        // Create a JDBC statement from the connection
        statement = connection.createStatement();
        // Execute the SQL
        results = statement.executeQuery(sql);
        // Get the meta data
        meta = results.getMetaData();
        // Make sure we got a row!
        if( !results.next() ) {
            throw new PersistenceException("No rows found!");
        }
        // For each column in the result set
        for(int i=1; i<=meta.getColumnCount(); i++) {
            // Put the value in the Hashtable using the column name
            // as a key
            h.put(meta.getColumnLabel(i), results.getObject(i));
        }
        // Call the restore from Hashtable method in the Persistent
        p.restore(trans, h);
    }
    catch( SQLException e ) {
        if( statement != null ) { // This is not required
            try { statement.close(); }
            catch( SQLException e2 ) { }
        }
        throw new PersistenceException(e);
    }
}
```

Example 6-7. DatabasePeer.java (continued)

```
    // Because JDBC allows all statements that modify the database to
    // go through the executeUpdate() method in java.sql.Statement,
    // we can encapsulate all of the persistence operations inside
    // a single method after we get the specific SQL.  This private
    // method takes any random SQL designed to modify the database
    // and executes it.
    private void save(DatabaseTransaction trans, String sql)
    throws PersistenceException {
        Connection connection = null;
        Statement statement = null;

        try {
            connection = trans.getConnection(); // Get the JDBC connection
            statement = connection.createStatement(); // Create a statement
            statement.executeUpdate(sql); // Execute the SQL
            statement.close(); // Close the statement (not required)
        }
        catch( SQLException e ) {
            if( statement != null ) { // not required
                try { statement.close(); }
                catch( SQLException e2) { }
            }
            throw new PersistenceException(e);
        }
    }


    /**
     * This method implements the update persistence operation
     * as prescribed by the PersistentPeer interface.  It asks
     * its subclasses for the proper SQL and then triggers
     * a save using that SQL statement.
     * @param p the persistent object to be updated
     * @param t the DatabaseTransaction to use for updating the object
     * @exception imaginary.persist.PersistenceException An error occurred
     * in updating the object in the database.
     */
    public void update(Persistent p, Transaction t)
    throws PersistenceException {
        save((DatabaseTransaction)t, getUpdateSql(p));
    }
}
```

This class is all about getting SQL from its application-specific subclass and then passing it through either `executeQuery()` or `executeUpdate()` in `java.sql.Statement`. In order to get the proper SQL, it prescribes four methods that subclasses implement to provide it with the proper application-specific SQL. We show how they get implemented when we get into the banking classes later in the chapter. Once it has the SQL, the method uses straight JDBC code for performing queries or updates using embedded SQL.

It would work even better to use stored procedures inside the DatabasePeer class. For the persistence library, however, I chose to use embedded SQL both due to limitations of mSQL—such as its lack of support for stored procedures—and the fact that stored procedure syntax can vary among JDBC drivers.

The last class required for a complete database persistence library is the DatabaseSetPeer class. Its job is actually much simpler than that of the DatabasePeer. It needs to grab SQL and pass it through executeQuery() in the Statement class. The twist is that it handles result sets containing multiple rows. In addition, subclasses need to be able to build SQL based on search criteria passed through a Hashtable. For example, if you wanted all accounts belonging to customer #559213, the Hashtable would contain the key cust_id with a value of 559213. The DatabaseSetPeer subclass would then know to build the following SQL:

```
SELECT * from t_accounts
WHERE cust_id = 559213;
```

The DatabaseSetPeer class imposes no interpretation on the values in that Hashtable. You can use them in any way you like to build SQL. Later in the chapter, we will build AccountSetPeer and CustomerSetPeer classes that build SQL based on search criteria. Example 6-8 provides the source code for the DatabaseSetPeer class.

Example 6-8. DatabaseSetPeer.java

```
/**
 * The DatabaseSetPeer performs database queries on behalf of
 * PersistentSet sets.
 */
package imaginary.persist;

import java.sql.Connection;
import java.sql.ResultSet;
import java.sql.ResultSetMetaData;
import java.sql.SQLException;
import java.sql.Statement;
import java.util.Hashtable;

public abstract class DatabaseSetPeer implements PersistentSetPeer {
    /**
     * Subclasses must implement this method to provide the
     * DatabaseSetPeer with the name of a subclass of Persistent
     * to instantiate for each row returned from the database.
```

Example 6-8. DatabaseSetPeer.java (continued)

```
 * @param h the Hashtable of values returned from the database query
 * @return the name of the class to instantiate for this row
 */
public abstract String getPersistentClass(Hashtable h);

/**
 * Subclasses must implement this method to provide the
 * DatabaseSetPeer with the proper SQL for performing a query.
 * The Hashtable may be null.
 * @param h a list of values with which to limit the query
 * @return the proper SELECT SQL for this set
 */
public abstract String getSql(Hashtable h);

/**
 * Implementation of the PersistentSetPeer method for restoring
 * a set without query criteria.
 * @param set the set being restored
 * @param trans the transaction to use for the restore
 * @exception imaginary.persist.PersistenceException An error
 * occurred restoring from the database.
 * @see imaginary.persist.PersistentSetPeer#restore
 */
public void restore(PersistentSet set, Transaction trans)
throws PersistenceException {
    restore(set, trans, null);
}


/**
 * Implementation of the PersistentSetPeer method for restoring
 * based on specified query criteria
 * @param set the set being restored
 * @param trans the transaction to use for the restore
 * @param data the query criteria
 * @exception imaginary.persist.PersistenceException An error
 * occurred restoring from the database.
 * @see imaginary.persist.PersistentSetPeer#restore
 */
public void restore(PersistentSet set, Transaction trans,
                    Hashtable data)
throws PersistenceException {
    ResultSetMetaData meta = null;
    Connection connection = null;
    Statement statement = null;
    ResultSet results = null;
    String sql = getSql(data); // Get the SQL from the subclass

    try {
```

Example 6-8. DatabaseSetPeer.java (continued)

```java
            // Get the Connection from the DatabaseTransaction
            connection = ((DatabaseTransaction)trans).getConnection();
            // Create a Statement from the Connection
            statement = connection.createStatement();
            // Get the results
            results = statement.executeQuery(sql);
            // Get the meta data
            meta = results.getMetaData();
            // While there are rows in the result set
            while( results.next() ) {
                Hashtable h = new Hashtable(); // Store the results here
                String class_name;
                Persistent p;

                // For each column in the row
                for(int i=1; i<=meta.getColumnCount(); i++) {
                    Object ob = results.getObject(i); // Get the value

                    h.put(meta.getColumnLabel(i), ob); // Stick it in
                                                       // Hashtable
                }
                // Get the name of the class to create from this row
                class_name = getPersistentClass(h);
                // Get a Persistent from the Persistent
                p = Persistent.getPersistent(trans, h, class_name);
                // Add the Persistent to the set
                set.addPersistent(p);
            }
            statement.close(); // closing statement closes results
            connection.commit(); // Release database locks
        }
        catch( SQLException e ) {
            if( statement != null ) {
                try { statement.close(); } // closes results too
                catch( SQLException e2 ) { }
            }
            throw new PersistenceException(e);
        }
    }
}
```

Here you see how the `DatabaseSetPeer` lets the `Persistent` class method `getPersistent()` worry about instantiating persistent objects. For each row it grabs from the database, the `DatabaseSetPeer` gets a class name for the row and then passes the information to the `Persistent`. Using this information, `Persistent` will either return an existing version of the object from memory or create a new one.

The Banking Classes

All of the banking classes are simple and straightforward. The business objects—Customer, Account, SavingsAccount, and CheckingAccount—all contain methods for restoring from a Hashtable and setting an ID based on a Hashtable. They know nothing else about how they are stored. The rest of what they do is specific to what kind of object they are and how they operate within the banking business. While I am not going to provide the source for each one of these classes here, we will take a look at the most important business object to the bank, the customer.

Example 6-9. Customer.java, the Customer Business Object

```
/**
 * This class is the business object that represents a bank customer.
 */
package bank.server;

import imaginary.persist.PersistenceException;
import imaginary.persist.Persistent;
import imaginary.persist.PersistentPeer;
import imaginary.persist.RemotePersistent;
import imaginary.persist.RemoteLockHolder;
import imaginary.persist.Transaction;
import java.util.Hashtable;

public class Customer extends Persistent {
    // Only one peer is needed to share among customers
    static private final CustomerPeer peer        = new CustomerPeer();

    // A set of all accounts belonging to this customer
    private AccountSet               accounts   = null;
    // The customer's first name
    private String                   first_name = null;
    // The customer's last name
    private String                   last_name  = null;

    /**
     * Constructs a new Customer.
     */
    public Customer() {
        super();
    }

    /**
     * Each customer has one or more accounts stored in an account set.
     * This method provides those accounts in an array format.
     * @return an array of customer accounts
```

Example 6-9. Customer.java, the Customer Business Object (continued)

```java
    */
    public Account[] getAccounts() {
        // getPersistents() is all the synchronization we need
        Persistent[] obs = accounts.getPersistents();
        Account[] accts = new Account[obs.length];

        // This trick is needed to make a Persistent[] an Account[]
        // since you cannot cast from one array type to another
        for(int i=0; i<obs.length; i++) {
            accts[i] = (Account)obs[i];
        }
        return accts;
    }


    /**
     * @return the AccountSet of accounts for this customer
     */
    public synchronized AccountSet getAccountSet() {
        return accounts;
    }


    /**
     * @return the customer's first name
     */
    public synchronized String getFirstName() {
        return first_name;
    }


    /**
     * The Persistent interface mandates that implementors
     * provide a setId(Hashtable) method that pulls the ID out of
     * a Hashtable and calls setId(int).
     * @param h a Hashtable of values from the data store
     * @see imaginary.persist.Persistent#setId
     */
    public synchronized void setId(Hashtable h) {
        // CustomerPeer defines the key for cust_id in the data store
        setId(((Integer)h.get(CustomerPeer.CUST_ID)).intValue());
    }


    /**
     * @return the customer's last name
     */
    public synchronized String getLastName() {
        return last_name;
    }


    /**
```

Example 6-9. Customer.java, the Customer Business Object (continued)

```
 * @return this object's PersistentPeer
 */
protected synchronized PersistentPeer getPersistentPeer() {
    return Customer.peer;
}

/**
 * The Customer implementation of the Persistent interface's
 * restore() method.  This takes a Hashtable of values and assigns
 * them to attributes in the Customer object.
 * @param trans the Transaction being used for the restore
 * @param data the Hashtable of data pulled from the data store
 * @exception imaginary.persist.PersistenceException An error occurred
 * restoring the Customer
 */
public synchronized void restore(Transaction trans, Hashtable data)
throws PersistenceException {
    Hashtable hash = new Hashtable();

    /*
     * Depending on your data store and table structure, the
     * Hashtable may have different keys
     */
    // Set the ID
    setId(((Integer)data.get(CustomerPeer.CUST_ID)).intValue());
    // Set the last name
    last_name = (String)data.get(CustomerPeer.LAST_NAME);
    // Set the first name
    first_name = (String)data.get(CustomerPeer.FIRST_NAME);
    // Create an account set
    accounts = new AccountSet();
    // Create a Hashtable that tells the AccountSet what customer ID
    // to use for restoring the accounts
    hash.put("cust_id", new Integer(getId()));
    // Restore all accounts for this customer
    accounts.restore(trans, hash);
}
}
```

For the purposes of this sample application, we will not be modifying customer objects, so Customer has no code for modifying customer data. It contains only attributes, the methods for accessing them, and the methods required by the Persistent class. Similarly, a business object peer for database persistence is nothing more than an SQL statement generator. Example 6-10 shows the code for the CustomerPeer that supports the database access for the Customer class.

Example 6-10. CustomerPeer.java

```java
/**
 * The CustomerPeer handles database access for the Customer business
 * object.  The DatabasePeer that it extends specifically prescribes
 * for it methods that allow it to create SQL statements.
 */
import imaginary.persist.Persistent;

public class CustomerPeer extends imaginary.persist.DatabasePeer {
    /**
     * The column header for the customer ID field in the t_customer table
     */
    static public final String CUST_ID    = "t_customer.cust_id";

    /**
     * The column header for the last_name field in the t_customer table
     */
    static public final String FIRST_NAME = "t_customer.first_name";

    /**
     * The column header for the last name field in the t_customer table
     */
    static public final String LAST_NAME  = "t_customer.last_name";

    /**
     * Provides the SQL used to insert a customer object into the database.
     * @param p the Customer being inserted
     * @return the SQL to insert the customer
     */
    protected String getInsertSql(Persistent p) {
        Customer cust = (Customer)p;        // Cast it to a Customer
        int cust_id = cust.getId();         // The customer id
        String last = cust.getLastName();   // The last name
        String first = cust.getFirstName(); // The first name

        // INSERT INTO t_customer (cust_id, last_name, first_name)
        // VALUES (1, 'the Clown', 'Bozo')
        return "INSERT INTO t_customer (cust_id, last_name, first_name) " +
            "VALUES (" + cust_id + ", '" + last + "', '" + first +
            "')";
    }

    /**
     * Provides the SQL used to delete a customer from the database
     * @param p the Customer being deleted
     * @return the SQL used to delete the customer
     */
    public String getRemoveSql(Persistent p) {
        // DELETE FROM t_customer WHERE cust_id = 1
```

Example 6-10. CustomerPeer.java (continued)

```
        return "DELETE FROM t_customer WHERE cust_id = " + p.getId();
    }

    /**
     * Provides the SQL used to restore a customer from the database
     * @param p the Customer being restored (only ID field is filled in)
     * @return the SQL used to restore that customer
     */
    public String getRestoreSql(Persistent p) {
        // SELECT * from t_customer WHERE cust_id = 1
        return "SELECT * from t_customer WHERE cust_id = " +
            p.getId();
    }

    /**
     * Provides the SQL used to update a customer in the database
     * @param p the Customer being updated
     * @return the SQL used to UPDATE that customer
     */
    public String getUpdateSql(Persistent p) {
        Customer cust = (Customer)p;               // Cast p to Customer
        int cust_id = cust.getId();                // Get the cust_id
        String last_name = cust.getLastName();     // Get the last name
        String first_name = cust.getFirstName();   // Get the first name

        // UPDATE t_customer
        // SET last_name  = 'the Clown',
        //     first_name = 'Bozo'
        // WHERE cust_id  = 1
        return "UPDATE t_customer " +
            "SET last_name = '" + last_name + "', " +
            "first_name = '" + first_name + "' " +
            "WHERE cust_id = " + cust_id;
    }
}
```

The Customer example should help you better see how a `Persistent` object works with its peers. The last step to understanding all of the pieces of the persistence library is to look at how sets work. Because they only handle restores, sets and their peers are very simple. The sole job of the set is to point to its peer. It therefore has only the single method, `getPersistentSetPeer()`, which is provided in Example 6-11.

Example 6-11. AccountSet.java

```
import imaginary.persist.PersistentSet;
import imaginary.persist.PersistentSetPeer;
```

Example 6-11. AccountSet.java (continued)

```java
public class AccountSet extends PersistentSet {
    // We only need one copy of an account set peer to handle the work
    // for all account sets, so make it static.
    static final AccountSetPeer peer = new AccountSetPeer();

    /**
     * Provides the PersistentSet with the peer to use
     * for data store access.
     */
    public PersistentSetPeer getPersistentSetPeer() {
        return AccountSet.peer;
    }
}
```

The peer, on the other hand, provides the class name to instantiate for each account and the SQL for restoring accounts.

`AccountSetPeer` actually performs a little trick so that it instantiates a `SavingsAccount` object for savings accounts and a `CheckingAccount` object for checking accounts. Example 6-12 shows how it does this.

Example 6-12. AccountSetPeer.java

```java
/**
 * The AccountSetPeer provides the runtime class name for the accounts
 * it is responsible for as well as the SQL for restoring them.
 */
import imaginary.persist.PersistentSet;
import imaginary.persist.Transaction;
import java.util.Hashtable;

public class AccountSetPeer extends imaginary.persist.DatabaseSetPeer {
    /**
     * Depending on the account type for the account being restored,
     * this method will return either "CheckingAccount" or
     * "SavingsAccount".
     * @param h the values from the database
     * @return the class name to instantiate for this row
     */
    public String getPersistentClass(Hashtable h) {
        String tmp = (String)h.get(AccountPeer.ACCOUNT_TYPE);

        if( tmp.equals("C") ) {
            return "CheckingAccount";
        }
        else {
            return "SavingsAccount";
        }
```

Example 6-12. AccountSetPeer.java (continued)

```
    }

    /**
     * Provides the proper SQL SELECT statement based on the values
     * that come from a database row stored in the Hashtable.  If the
     * Hashtable is null, all accounts are retrieved.
     * If a customer ID is passed, then all accounts for that customer
     * ID are provided.
     * @param h a Hashtable containing the customer ID
     * @return the SELECT SQL to get the accounts from the database with
     */
    public String getSql(Hashtable h) {
        if( h == null ) { // If no query criteria are specified
            return "SELECT * from t_accounts";
        }
        else {
            String tmp = "SELECT * from t_accounts WHERE ";
            int cust_id = -1;

            // SELECT * from t_accounts
            // WHERE cust_id = 1
            if( h.containsKey("cust_id") ) {
                cust_id = ((Integer)h.get("cust_id")).intValue();
            }
            return tmp + "cust_id = " + cust_id;
        }
    }
}
```

We have covered a lot of code in this chapter. By this point, you should feel comfortable with using JDBC and have a good feel for how it can be used inside a persistence library. It is important to remember that the ultimate goal of your database application is not to access a database. Instead, your application merely uses a database to solve a specific problem. The persistence library should therefore allow you to worry about solving that problem without worrying about database issues.

Of course, this persistence library is not an industrial strength class library that you can take immediately and use in mission-critical applications. The code we have discussed in this chapter is simply designed to show you how such a class library can work. Among other things, it is not designed for efficiency. A real persistence library would include code to allow partial restores of objects on demand. It would also include garbage-collection code so that persistent objects no longer in use are dereferenced (and thus reclaimed by the Java garbage-collector).

7

The User Interface

We say that error is appearance. This is false. On the contrary,
appearance is always true if we confine ourselves to it. Appearance is being.
—Jean-Paul Sartre
Truth and Existence

Appearance is truth. Whatever data you have stored in your database, it is what your users see that ultimately matters. As we explored previous chapters, a two-tier application creates copies of database data on the client. The database can change and leave the client with a different set of data from that sitting in the database. The users, however, continue to interface with the client under the belief that what they see is reality.

We have been through the hardest part of this application: the abstraction of application functionality into reusable components. Our tasks get easier and less tangled from here. We want to create a user interface that is not a copy of the data in the business objects, but a mirror of the business objects themselves. We want to know that whatever the users sees on the screen reflects the state of the business object at that instant. In Chapter 3, I presented a design for client interaction that treats the client as a system of business object observers. We will now dive into the details of that design and see how it plays out in the Java environment.

Observers and Observables

Earlier in the book, we talked about the observer pattern in object-oriented design. I used the Java AWT implementation of `Image` and `ImageObserver` as an example of how this pattern works. In object-oriented client/server development, our clients are observers of business objects in the same way as an

`ImageObserver` is an observer of `Image`. Take, for example, the window in Figure 7-1.

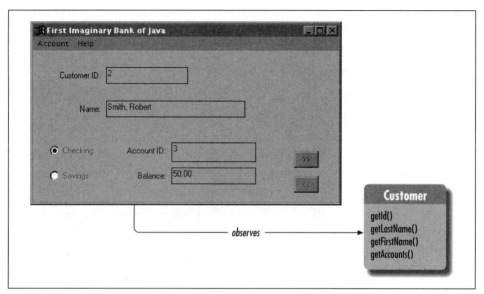

Figure 7-1. The customer window for the banking application observes a customer

This window shows detailed information about a bank customer. The values displayed in the window are direct mappings to the attributes of a `Customer` business object and the fields that display those values are widgets within a Java panel. When this window creates the panel, it gets the attributes directly from the `Customer` object and begins observing the `Customer`. When any client—even ones using a different interface—makes a change to that `Customer`, the `Customer` sends notices to all of its observers. This notice allows each observer to reflect the change to the customer in the window.

The Java core libraries provide us with classes to capture the observer pattern—`java.util.Observer` and `java.util.Observable`. As the names imply, `Observer` is an interface implemented by objects observing classes that extend `Observable`. Because `Observable` is a class, it must be the base class to whatever objects you intend to make observable. This can prove restrictive if you really need to have a different base class. The pattern, however, is extremely simple and easy to emulate if you absolutely have no other choice. In fact, we will have to do just that in Chapter 8 in order to RMI-enable the application. Within our persistence library, however, `Persistent` and `PersistentSet` extend `Observable`, so we are ready to go.

`Observable` keeps track of objects—`Observer` implementations—that have stated an interest in changes occurring to the `Observable` object. `Observable` contains the following methods for managing its observer list:

- `void addObserver(Observer)`

- `int countObservers()`

- `void deleteObserver(Observer)`

- `void deleteObservers()`

When a change occurs to an observable object, it marks itself changed using the method `setChanged()`. Marking the object changed, however, does not notify the observers of the change. You have to explicitly call the `notifyObservers()` method.

This might sound odd at first, but `notifyObservers()` does not immediately notify all observers. It notifies the object's observers only if `setChanged()` has been called in the object. Why do you have to take two steps to do one thing? For control purposes. The `setChanged()` method is a protected method. Only an `Observable` can mark itself as changed. The `notifyObservers()` method, however, is `public` and allows anyone to call it. In short, other objects— like `Thread` objects—can ask the `Observable` to notify its observers, but the ultimate control is left in the `Observable` to decide when the news actually goes out.

The `Observer` interface is simple:

```
public interface Observer {
    public abstract void update(Observable target, Object arg);
}
```

Whenever `notifyObservers()` is called in an `Observable` and it has been marked as changed, the `Observable` calls `update()` in all of its observers. As an added bonus, you can even specify an argument to pass to those `update()` methods through `notifyObservers()`. You can do this by optionally passing any `Object` as an argument to `notifyObservers()`.

Example 7-1 highlights the `Persistent` code that takes care of observer notification.

Example 7-1. The Observer Notification Code in Persistent.java

```
protected synchronized void modify(RemoteLockHolder h)
throws LockException {
    // Someone is doing something they should not!
    if( lock != null ) {
        if( h.hashCode() != lock.getHolder().hashCode() ) {
            throw new LockException("Illegal attempt to modify " +
```

Example 7-1. The Observer Notification Code in Persistent.java (continued)

```
                                        "object without a lock.");
        }
    }
    // First modification!
    if( lock == null ) {
        lock = Lock.createLock(h, this);
    }
    // Add Persistent.MODIFIED to the bitmask
    modifications |= Persistent.MODIFIED;
    setChanged();
}

public synchronized void remove(RemoteLockHolder h) throws LockException {
    // Check for a lock
    if( lock != null ) {
        if( h.hashCode() != lock.getHolder().hashCode() ) {
            throw new LockException("Illegal attempt to delete object " +
                                    "without a lock.");
        }
    }
    // Create the lock if it does not exist
    if( lock == null ) {
        lock = Lock.createLock(h, this);
    }
    // Mark the object deleted
    modifications |= Persistent.DELETED;
    setChanged();
}

protected synchronized void monitorLock() throws LockException {
    // If we cared, we might add a last touched check in here
    // to have the lock timeout.
    // If so, we would throw a LockException.
    notifyObservers();
}
```

In just these three lines, we have everything necessary to ensure that any observer is made aware of any changes in a persistent object. The only thing that is not immediately obvious is why notifyObservers() occurs in monitorLock(). If you think back to Chapter 6, each Persistent spawns a lock thread when it is modified. This lock thread makes periodic calls to monitorLock(), which is responsible for doing maintenance of the Persistent while it is locked. This responsibility includes checking that the lock should be kept and notifying observers of changes to the object.

Why not call notifyObservers() immediately after each change? You don't want processing on one client to wait around for all observers spread out over the network to be notified. Handling observer notification in a separate thread allows changes to be reported to observers without affecting processing for any single client or the application server.

Mapping GUI Panels to Business Objects

As a user, you view business objects in two ways: individually and collectively. The customer window we discussed earlier shows information on a specific customer with all of the data on that customer's accounts. This user interface allows me to keep the code as simple as possible for demonstrating how observers work in a client/server application. Because an application may observe objects in either manner, I set up both `Persistent` and `PersistentSet` as observable objects in the persistence library.

Windows that observe persistent objects individually have a single panel that observes that object directly. On the other hand, windows that observe them collectively observe the sets of which they are part. These set panels in turn contain individual panels that view individual objects. Figure 7-2 provides a better look at how this works.

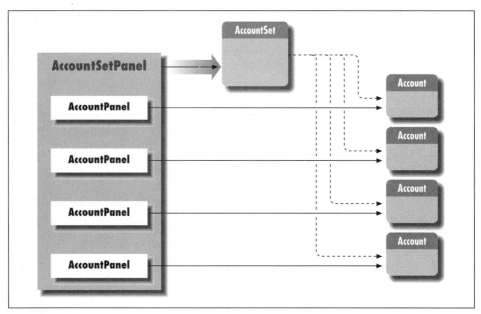

Figure 7-2. The mapping of Java panels to business objects

The one window in this teller front-end is actually made up of many panels. Some of these exist for aesthetic reasons; others for observing business objects. There are three observer panels in this window. The first panel observes the customer

selected when the user selects Open on the Accounts menu. The second panel
observes the same AccountSet shown in Figure 7-2 that belongs to the customer
observed by the first panel. Because the AccountSet is an attribute of the
Customer, the AccountSetPanel appears on the CustomerPanel. That
AccountSetPanel in turn contains zero or more instances of the third panel,
the one that observes an individual Account in the same way the first panel
observes a Customer.

Here we have another opportunity to take behavior common among client/server
applications and add GUI support to add to the persistence library. We have identified two distinct kinds of observer panels, individual and collective. Example 7-2
provides the source code for a PersistentPanel class that observes individual
persistent objects.

Example 7-2. PersistentPanel.java

```java
/**
 * The PersistentPanel class is a Java panel that observes changes in
 * Persistent instances.
 */
package imaginary.gui;

import imaginary.persist.RemoteLockHolder;
import imaginary.persist.Persistent;
import java.util.Observable;
import javautil.Observer;
import java.awt.Panel;

public abstract class PersistentPanel extends Panel
implements ChangeObserver, Observer {
    private RemoteLockHolder lock_holder = null;
    private Persistent observed    = null;

    public PersistentPanel(RemoteLockHolder h) {
        super();
        observed = null;
        lock_holder = h;
    }

    public PersistentPanel(RemoteLockHolder h, Persistent p) {
        super();
        observed = p;
        lock_holder = h;
        p.addObserver(this);
    }

    protected RemoteLockHolder getLockHolder() {
        return lock_holder;
```

Example 7-2. PersistentPanel.java (continued)

```
    }

    public Persistent getObserved() {
        return observed;
    }

    public void update(Observable target, Object args) {
        ChangeMonitor.postChange(this);
    }
}
```

This class does not really do a lot more than organize the way notices are sent to the panel. As an `Observer`, the panel receives change notifications through the `update()` method. For reasons that will be more apparent once we distribute the application using RMI in Chapter 8, the `PersistentPanel` cannot call methods in the observed `Persistent` from inside the same thread as `update()`. It instead uses the `ChangeMonitor` class to queue up the change notification and display the new information in a different thread. `ChangeMonitor` is simply a `Thread` that tracks which panels have seen a change. During each iteration through its `run()` loop, `ChangeMonitor` calls `observeChange()` (the only method prescribed by `ChangeObserver`) to allow the panel to display any changes. Example 7-3 shows the `PersistentPanel` implementation for an account.

Example 7-3. AccountPanel.java

```
/**
 * An AccountPanel displays information for a single bank account.
 */
package bank.client;

import bank.server.Account;
import bank.server.Customer;
import imaginary.gui.PersistentPanel;
import imaginary.persist.RemoteLockHolder;
import java.awt.Checkbox;
import java.awt.CheckboxGroup;
import java.awt.Label;
import java.awt.TextField;
import java.text.NumberFormat;
import java.util.Observable;

public class AccountPanel extends PersistentPanel {
    private TextField      balance_field = null;
    private Label          balance_label = null;
    private CheckboxGroup cb_group       = null;
```

Example 7-3. AccountPanel.java (continued)

```java
private boolean       changed       = false;
private Checkbox      checking_cb   = null;
private TextField     id_field      = null;
private Label         id_label      = null;
private Checkbox      savings_cb    = null;

/********************* Constructors ***********************/
/**
 * Constructs a new AccountPanel associated with a specific
 * RemoteLockHolder.
 * @param h the RemoteLockHolder associated with this panel's edits
 */
public AccountPanel(RemoteLockHolder h) {
    super(h);
    createComponents();
}

/**
 * Constructs a new AccountPanel for the specified account.
 * @param h the RemoteLockHolder associated with this panel's edits
 * @param a the bank account to display
 */
public AccountPanel(RemoteLockHolder h, Account a)
    super(h, a);
    createComponents();
}

/**
 * Puts the panel's widgets on the panel
 */
public void createComponents() {
    setLayout(null);
    { // check boxes
        cb_group = new CheckboxGroup();
        checking_cb = new Checkbox("Checking", cb_group, false);
        checking_cb.enable(false);
        checking_cb.reshape(12,12,84,24);
        add(checking_cb);
        savings_cb = new Checkbox("Savings", cb_group, false);
        savings_cb.enable(false);
        savings_cb.reshape(12,48,84,24);
        add(savings_cb);
    }
    { // ID
        id_label = new Label("Account ID:",Label.RIGHT);
        id_label.reshape(96,12,88,24);
        add(id_label);
        id_field = new TextField();
```

Example 7-3. AccountPanel.java (continued)

```
        id_field.setEditable(false);
        id_field.reshape(192,12,124,28);
        add(id_field);
    }
    { // balance
        balance_label = new Label("Balance:",Label.RIGHT);
        balance_label.reshape(108,48,76,24);
        add(balance_label);
        balance_field = new TextField();
        balance_field.setEditable(false);
        balance_field.reshape(192,48,124,24);
        add(balance_field);
    }
    refresh();
}


/****************** Displaying data and cleaning up *************/
/**
 * This implements the ChangeObserver method inherited from
 * PersistentPanel.  PersistentPanel handles responding to changes in
 * the observed account.
 */
public void observeChange() {
    refresh();
}


/**
 * Displays current account data on the screen.
 */
public void refresh() {
    Observable o = getObserved();

    if( o == null ) {
        id_field.setText("");
        balance_field.setText("");
        checking_cb.setState(true);
        savings_cb.setState(false);
    }
    else {
        Account a = (Account)o;

        // This is the proper way to handle formatting in JDK 1.1
        NumberFormat f = NumberFormat.getCurrencyInstance();

        id_field.setText("" + a.getId());
        balance_field.setText(f.format(a.getBalance()));
        if( a.getAccountType().equals("C") ) {
            checking_cb.setState(true);
```

Example 7-3. AccountPanel.java (continued)

```
                savings_cb.setState(false);
            }
            else {
                checking_cb.setState(false);
                savings_cb.setState(true);
            }
        }
    }

    /**
     * When the window containing this is closed or the panel is
     * removed, it should call cleanUp() to clean up any observer
     * relationships.
     */
    protected void cleanUp() {
        Observable o = getObserved();

        if( o != null ) {
            o.deleteObserver(this);
        }
    }
}
```

Persistent Sets

Most applications, like this one, need to display objects not only individually, but also collectively. Sets differ from regular persistent objects in that there are only two kinds of changes they can undergo: deletions and additions. When we have a set of persistent objects that we are watching, we need to keep track of situations in which an object is added to the set or deleted from it. Because Java panels are containers that may contain other panels, we can create a special set panel that just worries about the deletes and updates. We leave the observation of members of the set to `PersistentPanel` objects that get placed on the set panel.

In the customer window, I placed the multiple accounts for each customer into an account set panel governed by the AWT `CardLayout` panel. A user can click on the forward and reverse buttons to flip through each of the `AccountPanel` objects in the `AccountSetPanel`. If an object gets added to or deleted from the set, the panel observing that object also gets added to or deleted from the panel observing the set.

In the application we are developing, `PersistentSetPanel` and `PersistentPanel` do not differ at all. As simple as our application is, they really perform the exact same functions and thus use the exact same routines. They are, however, conceptually different and would require different functionality in a more robust application. For example, we are not implementing anything that deletes from or adds to sets; additionally, adding to sets is certainly non-trivial. In order to handle additions, the update() method would need to receive a second argument signifying that the operation is an addition or deletion as well as which object is affected. The hard part, however, is getting the persistence library to let a set know when a new object has been added that might fit into the set. Given a newly created account, each set should be queried to see if that new account belongs in the set. We would thus have to write code so that Persistent also keeps track of all PersistentSet instances. Each time a new Persistent is created, you would then have Persistent call some method in each PersistentSet that tests to see if the new object should be a member.

The most complex component of the customer window is the class that implements PersistentSetPanel to observe the customer's accounts. Not only does it need to put the account panels together into a CardLayout, but it also needs to create a mechanism for navigating among those account panels. Due to the newness of JDK 1.1, the event handling that I use to do this may be new to you. Specifically, handling button presses is much easier with JDK 1.1 than it used to be. Instead of automatically triggering the action() method in a container for every action event whether or not the container has any interest in that event, objects can now express interest in action events in GUI components by implementing the ActionListener interface and by calling addAction Listener(this) on the desired component. In a constructor, for example, a window might add a button to a panel and then express its interest in button clicks:

```
public class SomeWindow extends Frame implements ActionListener {
    public SomeWindow() {
        super();
        Panel p = new Panel();
        Button b = new Button("Press Me");
        p.add(b);
        add(p);
        b.addActionListener(this);
    }
}
```

Later in the source code, the object would define an actionPerformed() method for handling the button click. If the window is watching multiple components, the object triggered can be accessed through the event.getSource() method.

```
public void actionPerformed(ActionEvent event) {
    // do whatever should happen here
}
```

Example 7-4 provides the source code for the `AccountSetPanel`.

Example 7-4. AccountSetPanel.java

```java
/**
 * A Java panel with a CardLayout that allows the user
 * to flip through accounts.
 */
package bank.client;

import bank.server.Account;
import bank.server.ccountSet;
import imaginary.gui.PersistentSetPanel;
import imaginary.persist.RemoteLockHolder;
import imaginary.persist.Persistent;
import imaginary.persist.PersistentSet;
import java.awt.Button;
import java.awt.CardLayout;
import java.awt.event.ActionEvent;
import java.awt.event.ActionListener;
import java.util.Observable;

public class AccountSetPanel extends PersistentSetPanel
implements ActionListener {
    // index of the currently displayed account panel
    private int           current_account = -1;
    // the button to navigate to the next panel
    private Button        next_button     = null;
    // the list of account panels being displayed by this set panel
    private AccountPanel[] panels         = null;
    // the button to navigate to the previous panel
    private Button        previous_button = null;

    /********************** Constructors **********************/
    /**
     * Creates a new AccountSetPanel.  The buttons array are the next
     * and previous buttons placed on the customer panel.  Visually,
     * they fit better on the customer panel.  They go here, however,
     * because this panel is interested in their events.
     * @param buttons the next and previous buttons in that order
     * @param h the lock holder for any modifications
     */
    public AccountSetPanel(Button[] buttons, RemoteLockHolder h)
        super(h);
        next_button = buttons[0];
        previous_button = buttons[1];
        createComponents();
    }

    /**
```

Example 7-4. AccountSetPanel.java (continued)

```
    * Constructs an AccountSetPanel observing the specified set.
    * @param buttons the next and previous buttons in that order
    * @param h the lock holder for any modifications
    * @param set the set being observed
    */
   public AccountSetPanel(Button[] buttons, RemoteLockHolder h,
               PersistentSet set)
       super(h, set);
       next_button = buttons[0];
       previous_button = buttons[1];
       createComponents();
   }


   /**
    * @return the account currently being viewed
    */
   public Account getSelectedAccount() {
       AccountPanel acct_panel = panels[current_account-1];

       return (Account)acct_panel.getObserved();
   }


   /**
    * Places the individual widgets on the panel.
    */
   protected void createComponents() {
       AccountSet set = (AccountSet)getObserved();
       Persistent[] accounts;

       // CardLayout allows us to view one account panel at a time.
       setLayout(new CardLayout(0,0));
       // Don't draw anything if no set is being observed.
       if( set == null ) {
           return;
       }
       accounts = set.getPersistents();
       current_account = 1;
       panels = new AccountPanel[accounts.length];
       // For each observed account, add an account panel.
       for(int i=0; i<accounts.length; i++) {
           panels[i] = new AccountPanel(getLockHolder(),
                                     (Account)accounts[i]);
           panels[i].reshape(insets().left + 24,insets().top +
                             132,384,120);
           add("" + i, panels[i]);
       }
       previous_button.addActionListener(this);
       previous_button.enable(false);
```

Example 7-4. AccountSetPanel.java (continued)

```
        next_button.addActionListener(this);
        if( panels.length < 2 ) {
            next_button.enable(false);
        }
    }


    /****************** Displaying data and cleaning up ************/
    /**
     * Implementation of the ChangeObserver method for handling changes
     * in observed objects.
     */
    public void observeChange() {
        // Since this application does not support the addition
        // or deletion of accounts, it will not actually
        // observe any changes.  If it did, however, you would use
        // this method to add new panels or remove deleted ones.
    }


    /**
     * When the window gets destroyed or this panel is removed,
     * cleanUp() gets called to allow the panel to remove itself
     * from the observer list of its set.
     */
    protected void cleanUp() {
        Observable o = getObserved();

        if( o != null ) {
            o.deleteObserver(this);
        }
        if( panels != null ) {
            for(int i=0; i<panels.length; i++) {
                panels[i].cleanUp();
            }
        }
    }


    /********************* Event handlers *******************/
    /**
     * This method is new to JDK 1.1.  It handles action events for
     * components this class has expressed interest in.  In the case
     * of the account set panel, we want to know when one of the buttons
     * is clicked.
     * @param event the triggered event
     */
    public void actionPerformed(ActionEvent event) {
        Button b = (Button)event.getSource();

        // the user clicked next
```

Example 7-4. AccountSetPanel.java (continued)

```
            if( b == next_button ) {
                // Flip to the next account in the card layout.
                ((CardLayout)getLayout()).next(this);
                current_account++;
                // If this is the last account, disable the next button.
                if( current_account == panels.length ) {
                    next_button.enable(false);
                }
                // If this is not the first account, enable the previous button.
                if( current_account > 1 ) {
                    previous_button.enable(true);
                }
            }
            else {
                // Flip to the previous account in the card layout.
                ((CardLayout)getLayout()).previous(this);
                current_account--;
                // If this is the first account, disable the previous button.
                if( current_account < 2 ) {
                    previous_button.enable(false);
                }
                // If this is not the last account, enable the next button.
                if( current_account < panels.length ) {
                    next_button.enable(true);
                }
            }
        }
    }
}
```

We now have both the back-end objects and the user interface to support a simple banking application. Nevertheless, we are missing a means for the user interface to communicate with the server. In fact, I have so far constructed the entire system as if it were running on the same virtual machine. In the next chapter we will cover RMI, the tool to make the client and application server talk without changing this single-system architecture. At that point, we will have a complete application that allows users to view account information and transfer funds between accounts.

8

Remote Objects

Objects contain the possibility of all situations.
—Ludwig Wittgenstein
Tractatus Logico Philisophicus

I have already mentioned one of the Java mantras: "write once, compile once, run anywhere." You may have heard another very important one: "the network is the computer." The Web is based on the principle that information resources may be found all over the Internet. Your browser enables you to access all of this information as if it were on your desktop. "The network is the computer," however, refers to more than the ability to access information resources anywhere in the world. It means being able to access and utilize applications and computing resources anywhere in the world. It means forgetting about the barriers that separate machines and treating them as one huge computer.

The object is the center of the Java world. If we are to truly look at client/server systems as single systems, we need a way to distribute Java objects across the network. Several technologies like CORBA (Common Object Request Broker Architecture) already exist to enable developers to distribute objects across a network. CORBA has a very wide reach and is wrought with complexities associated with its grandiose goals. For example, it supports applications whose distributed components are written in different languages. In order to support everything from writing an object interface in C to handling more traditional object languages like Java and Smalltalk, it has built up an architecture with a very steep learning curve.

CORBA does its job very well, but it does a lot more than you need in a pure Java environment. This extra functionality has a cost in terms of programming complexity. Unlike other programming languages, Java has distributed support built into its core. Borrowing heavily from CORBA, Java supports a simpler pure-

Java distributed object solution called Remote Method Invocation (RMI). In this chapter, we will use RMI to provide a communications solution for three-tier client/server applications.

Traditional Client/Server Interaction

The banking application we have so far constructed has no way for the client and server to communicate with each other. In fact, the only way you can get the system we have in place to work is by running it stand-alone. That's hardly a three-tier system. In order to move the application to three tiers, we need to split apart the client and application server and provide those two layers with a communications protocol.

On the Internet, IP-based sockets handle all network communications. A client/server application in that environment requires a complex protocol on top of those IP sockets to structure the data in a format both sides will understand. A host of protocols like HTTP and FTP exist to provide a structure for specific Internet applications. But these protocols exist with very narrow purposes in mind and would not suit an application such as ours.

We could write our own socket communication protocol. For an account transfer, for example, we could send a stream of data to the server that says which account is the source, which one is the target, and how much is being transferred. The code might look something like this:

```
void transfer(int id_orig, int id_targ, float amount)
throws SomeObscureProtocolException {
    int status;

    socket_output.writeInt(Account.TRANSFER); // signifies what kind
                                               // of operation
    socket_output.writeInt(id_orig);
    socket_output.writeInt(id_targ);
    socket_output.writeFloat(amount);
    status = socket_input.readInt();
    if( status != 0 ) {
        throw new SomeObscureProtocolException(status);
    }
}
```

On the other end, we would have some object that listens to the socket for new bank transactions and pulls data off the connection based on the transaction type. You would have to do all of this work for an operation that does nothing more than a `account.transfer(amount, target)` call—except that `account` and `target` are objects located somewhere else on the network.

Distributed object specifications like CORBA and RMI provide protocols that reduce client/server communication to method calls. Your application calls `account.transfer(amount, target)`, and something under the covers recognizes `account` as a remote object and sends the call across the network to the real `transfer()` method in the real `account` object.

The greatest conceptual difference between remote and local method calls is that things can go wrong for remote calls that do not apply to local ones. The most obvious thing that can happen is that the connection between the client and server can go down. For this reason and others, you will need to carefully plan and understand which objects and methods can be called remotely. In addition, you need to be able to handle the special problems that can arise for remote method calls.

The Structure of RMI

RMI is an API that lets you mostly ignore the fact that your objects are distributed across a network. While you do need to take into account how the objects are distributed at design time, your method calls treat remote methods almost identically to the way they treat local ones. The biggest problem with providing this sort of API is that you are dealing with two separate virtual machines existing in two separate address spaces. Take, for example, the situation where you have a `Bat` object that calls `hit()` in a `Ball` instance. Located together on the same virtual machine, the method call looks like this:

```
ball.hit();
```

We want RMI to provide us with the exact same syntax when the `Bat` instance is on a client machine and the `Ball` on a server. The problem is that the `Ball` instance does not exist inside the client's memory. How can I possibly trigger an event in an object to which I have no reference? The first step is to get a reference.

Access to Remote Objects

I am going to co-opt the term *server* for a minute and use it to refer to the virtual machine that holds the real copies of one or more distributed objects. In a distributed object system, you can have a single host (generally the application server) act as an object server—a place from which clients get remote objects—or you can have all of the systems act as object servers. Clients simply need to be aware of where the object servers are located. An object server has a single defining function: to make objects available to remote clients.*

---

* Of course, our application server is doing the object server work. Thus, in addition to serving objects, the application server is doing things like database access and other functions we have so far built into it.

A special program that comes with the JDK called `rmiregistry` listens to a port on the object server's machine. The object server in turn binds object instances to that port using a special URL so it can be found by clients later. The format of the RMI URL is `rmi://server/object`. A client then uses that URL to find a desired object. For the ball example above, the ball would be bound to the URL `rmi://athens.imaginary.com/Ball`. An object server binds an object to a URL by calling the `static rebind()` method of `java.rmi.Naming`.

```
Naming.rebind("rmi://athens.imaginary.com/Ball", new Ball());
```

Of course, the `rmi://athens.imaginary.com/` portion of the URL above is self-evident; you cannot bind an object instance to a URL on another machine. `Naming` allows you to rebind an object using only the object name for short:

```
Naming.rebind("Ball", new Ball());
```

NOTE   In RMI, binding is the process of associating an object with an RMI URL. The `rebind()` method specifically creates this association. At this point the object is registered with the `rmiregistry` application and available to client systems. Any reference by any system to its URL is thus specifically a reference to the bound object.

The `rebind()` methods make a specific object instance available to remote objects who do a lookup on the object's URL. This is where life gets complicated. When a client connects to the object URL, it cannot get the object bound to that URL. That object exists only in the memory of the server. The client needs a way to fool itself into thinking it has the object while routing all method calls in that object over to the real object. RMI uses Java interfaces to provide this sort of hocus pocus.

Remote Interfaces

All Java objects that you intend to make available as distributed objects must implement an interface that extends the RMI interface `java.rmi.Remote`. We call this making an object remote. You might do a quick double-take if you glance at the `java.rmi.Remote` source code. It looks like this:

```
package java.rmi;

public interface Remote {
}
```

No, there is no typo there. The interface specifies no methods to be implemented. It exists so that objects in the virtual machines on both the local and remote systems have a common base class they can use for deriving to all remote objects. They need this base class since the RMI methods look for subclasses of `Remote` as arguments.

When you write a remote object, you have to create an interface that extends `Remote` and specify all methods that can be called remotely. In the bat and ball example, we might have had the following interface:

```
public interface RemoteBall extends java.rmi.Remote {
    public abstract void hit() throws java.rmi.RemoteException;
    public abstract int getPosition() throws RemoteException;
}
```

We then write the `Ball` class so that it implements `RemoteBall`. Ball might look like:

```
import java.rmi.RemoteException;
import java.rmi.server.UnicastRemoteObject;

public class Ball extends UnicastRemoteObject implements RemoteBall {
    private int position = 0;

    public Ball() throw RemoteException {
        super();
    }

    public int getPosition() {
        return position;
    }

    public void hit() {
        position += calculateDistance();
    }

    protected int calculateDistance() {
        return 10;
    }
}
```

The `java.rmi.server.UnicastRemoteObject` class that the `Ball` extends provides support for exporting the ball; that is, it allows the virtual machine to make it available to remote systems. This may look like what the `Naming` class does, but it has a different purpose. `Naming` ensures that the object is bound to a particular URL, while exporting an object enables it to be passed across the network. This means that you can pass the object as a method argument or return it as a return value. It also means you can use `Naming.rebind()` to make the object available through a URL lookup. A URL lookup looks like this:

```
ball(RemoteBall)Naming.lookup("rmi://athens.imaginnary.-com/Ball");
```

Because you may not have the option of extending `UnicastRemoteObject`—
we will not have this option in the banking application—you can export your
objects another way using the following syntax in the object constructor:

```
public Ball() throws RemoteException {
    super();
    UnicastRemoteObject.exportObject(this);
}
```

After writing both classes, we compile them just like any other object. This will of
course generate two *.class* files, `RemoteBall.class` and `Ball.class`.

The final step in making the `Ball` class distributed is to run the RMI compiler,
rmic, against it. In this case, run *rmic* using the following command line:

```
rmic Ball
```

Like the `java` command and unlike the `javac` command, `rmic` takes a fully
qualified class name as an argument. That means if we had the `Ball` class in a
package called `baseball`, we would run `rmic` as:

```
rmic -dclassdir baseball.Ball
```

In this case, *classdir* represents whatever the root directory for your `base-
ball` package class files is. This will likely be one of the directories in your
CLASSPATH. The output of `rmic` will be two classes, `Ball_Skel.class` (the
skeleton) and `Ball_Stub.class` (the stub). These classes will be placed relative
to the *classdir* you specified on the command line.

Stubs and Skeletons

I have introduced a couple of concepts, stub and skeleton, without any explanation. They are two objects you should never have to concern yourself with, but
they perform all of the magic that makes a remote method call work. In
Figure 8-1, I show where these two objects fit in a remote method call.

The process of translating a remote method call into network format is called
marshaling; the reverse is called unmarshaling. When you run the `rmic`
command on your remote-enabled classes, it generates two classes that perform
the tasks of marshaling and unmarshaling. The first of these is the stub object, a
special object that implements all of the remote interfaces implemented by its
remote object. The difference is that where the remote object actually performs
the business logic associated with a method, the stub takes the arguments to the
method and sends them across the network to the skeleton object on the server.
In other words, it marshals the method parameters and sends them to the server.
The skeleton object, in turn, unmarshals those parameters; it takes the raw data

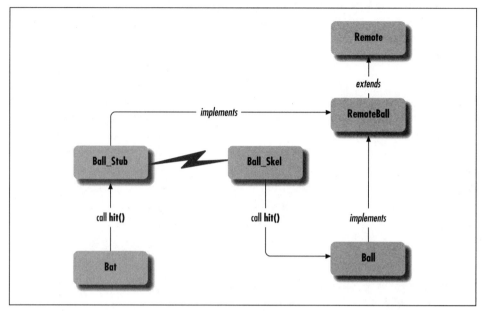

Figure 8-1. The process of calling a method in a remote object

from the network, translates it into Java objects, and then calls the proper method in the remote object.

The skeleton and stub perform the reverse roles for return values. The skeleton takes the return value from the method and sends it across the network. The client stub then takes the socket data and turns it into Java data, returning it to the calling method.

The Special Exception: java.rmi.RemoteException

All methods that can be called remotely as well as all constructors for remote objects must throw a special exception called `java.rmi.RemoteException`. The methods you write will never explicitly throw this exception. Instead, the local virtual machine will throw it when you encounter a network error during a remote method call.

A `RemoteException` is unlike any other exception. When you write an application to be run on a single virtual machine, you know that if your code is solid, you can predict potential exception situations and where they might occur. You can count on no such thing with a `RemoteException`. It can happen at any time during the course of a remote method call, and you may have no way of knowing why it happened. You therefore need to write your application code with the knowledge that at any point your code can fail for no discernible reason at all and

have contingencies to support such failures. We will definitely need to be able to
handle this in the banking application.

The Object Server

One of the things you cannot do through RMI is create a remote object on the
object server at will; you cannot do a remote equivalent to new. In a well-designed
distributed system, however, you do not need to do this. Instead, you should only
need to rebind one or two objects that give a client access to all other remote
objects on the object server. For example, in the banking application, I will create
an AppServer object that makes itself available to clients for serving Customer
objects. Each client can then use the Customer object to get all Account objects
associated with the Customer. Example 8-1 shows the AppServer code.

Example 8-1. AppServer.java

```
/**
 * The application server for the banking application.
 * This makes itself available to clients which can use it to get
 * references to client objects.
 */
package bank.server;

import imaginary.persist.DatabaseTransaction;
import imaginary.persist.PersistenceException;
import imaginary.persist.Persistent;
import imaginary.persist.RemoteLockHolder;
import imaginary.persist.Transaction;
import java.rmi.Naming;
import java.rmi.RemoteException;
import java.rmi.server.UnicastRemoteObject;
import java.util.Properties;
import java.rmi.RMISecurityManager;

public class AppServer extends UnicastRemoteObject implements
RemoteAppServer {
    /**
     * The entry point to the application server.
     * It takes three arguments:<BR>
     * <OL>
     * <LI> The data store URL
     * <LI> The user ID used to connect to the data store
     * <LI> The password used to connect to the data store
     * </OL>
     * It then makes an instance of the AppServer class available to
     * all connecting clients via the RMI URL:<BR>
     * rmi://host/AppServer
     * @param args the args to the AppServer process
```

Example 8-1. AppServer.java (continued)

```
    */
    static public void main(String[] args) {
        if( args.length != 3 ) {
          System.out.println("Syntax: [java AppServer URL UID PASSWORD]");
            return;
        }
        System.out.println("Installing the security manager...");
        System.setSecurityManager(new RMISecurityManager());
        try {
            AppServer server;
            Properties props = new Properties();
            String url = args[0];

            props.put("user", args[1]);
            props.put("password", args[2]);
            System.out.println("Starting the application server...");
            Naming.rebind("AppServer", new AppServer(url, props));
            System.out.println("AppServer bound with url: " + url + "...");
        }
        catch( Exception e ) {
            e.printStackTrace();
        }
    }

    /**
     * Constructs a new AppServer object.  There should be only one
     * per application server process.
     * @param u the data store URL
     * @param props the properties containing the user ID and password
     * @exception java.rmi.RemoteException thrown if the object cannot be
     * exported
     */
    public AppServer(String u, Properties props) throws RemoteException {
        super();
        Transaction.url = u;
        Transaction.properties = props;
    }

    /**
     * Provides a remote client with a reference to a customer object
     * located on the application server.
     * @param h the lock holder on the client
     * @param id the customer ID for the desired customer object
     * @exception imaginary.persist.PersistenceException an error occurred
     * restoring the desired customer
     * @exception java.rmi.RemoteException an error occurred exporting the
     * customer
     */
```

Example 8-1. AppServer.java (continued)

```
public RemoteCustomer getCustomer(RemoteLockHolder h, int id)
throws PersistenceException, RemoteException {
    Transaction t = Transaction.getTransaction();
    RemoteCustomer c;

    try {
        c = (RemoteCustomer)Persistent.getPersistent(t, id,
            "bank.server.Customer");
    }
    catch( Exception e ) {
        e.printStackTrace();
        return null;
    }
    return c;
    }
}
```

After running `rmic` on the `AppServer` and the other remote objects in the
system, you need to run `rmiregistry` before running the application server.
This program listens to port 1099 for client RMI requests. You can change this
port number if you like by specifying it at the command line. If you use an alter-
nate port, however, your RMI URLs should reflect that port: for instance,
rmi://athens.imaginary.com:1500/AppServer.

To connect with the application server, a client looks up the `AppServer` object:

```
RemoteAppServer server =

(RemoteAppServer)Naming.lookup("rmi://athens.imaginary.com/AppServer");
```

The application server is responsible for serving all business objects. Each client
shares this single `AppServer` instance from the application server. Using the
`getCustomer()` method, a client can query the AppServer instance to find
specific `Customer` objects. The important thing to note is that you can pass
around objects—remote and otherwise—through return values and as parameters
to methods once you have done a lookup on your first remote object. You just
cannot create remote objects like you can local ones.

Security

Security on an object server needs to worry about many of the same issues an
applet worries about. Specifically, you need a security manager to make sure that
you are not loading any nasty classes from clients across the network. In the App-
Server example, you saw me install the `java.rmi.RMISecurityManager`
class as the application server security manager. The `RMISecurityManager`
provides this level of security. If you fail to set the application server security

manager to `RMISecurityManager` (or a subclass), then RMI will load only stub classes from local files in the application server CLASSPATH.

Another security issue you will certainly encounter on the Internet is the use of firewalls; perhaps by your organization, certainly by clients. A remote method call requires opening a direct socket from the client to the server. You might think that this would ruin RMI for clients connecting from behind a firewall since they cannot open sockets to port 1099 (or whatever port you assign to `rmiregistry`). RMI takes this problem into account. If the client applet or application fails to make a connection using an RMI URL, it will tunnel through the HTTP port (80) disguised as a CGI call. This masquerade is handled entirely by the stubs and skeletons, so it is not something you need to worry about. You do have to keep in mind, however, that this kind of call works in only one direction. Because there is likely no HTTP daemon on the client, *you cannot make calls from an object server to a client behind a firewall.*

Object Serialization

Not all objects that you pass between virtual machines are remote. In fact, you need to be able to pass the primitive Java data types as well as many basic Java objects such as a `String` or a `Hashtable` that are not remote. When a non-remote object is passed across virtual machine boundaries, it gets passed by value using object serialization instead of the traditional Java way of passing objects, by reference. Object serialization is a feature of the Java 1.1 release that allows objects to be turned into a data stream that you can use in the same ways you can use any other Java streams—send it to a file, over a network, or to standard output. If we had implemented file system persistence in the persistence library, we would have used object serialization to save persistent objects to a file. What is important about this method of passing objects across virtual machines is that changes you make to the object on one virtual machine are not reflected in the other virtual machine.

Most of the core Java classes are serializable. If you wish to build classes that are not remote but need to be passed across virtual machines (this should be rare), you need to make those classes serializable. A serializable class minimally needs to implement `java.io.Serializable`. For almost any kind of non-sensitive data you might want to serialize, just implementing `Serializable` is enough. You do not even have to write a method; `Object` already handles the serialization for you. It will, however, assume that you don't want the object to be serializable unless you implement `Serializable`. Example 8-2 provides a simple example of how object serialization works. When you run it, you will see the `SerialDemo` instance in the second block display the values of one created in the first block.

Example 8-2. A Simple Demonstration of Object Serialization

```java
import java.io.*;

public class SerialDemo implements Serializable {
    static public void main(String[] args) {
        try {
            { // Save a SerialDemo object with a value of 5.
                FileOutputStream f = new FileOutputStream("/tmp/testing");
                ObjectOutputStream s = new ObjectOutputStream(f);
                SerialDemo d= new SerialDemo(5);

                s.writeObject(d);
                s.flush();
            }
            { // Now restore it and look at the value.
                FileInputStream f = new FileInputStream("/tmp/testing");
                ObjectInputStream s = new ObjectInputStream(f);
                SerialDemo d = (SerialDemo)s.readObject();

                System.out.println("SerialDemo.getVal() is: " +
                                    d.getVal());
            }
        }
        catch( Exception e ) {
            e.printStackTrace();
        }
    }

    int test_val= 7; // value defaults to 7

    public SerialDemo() {
        super();
    }

    public SerialDemo(int x) {
        super();
        test_val = x;
    }

    public int getVal() {
        return test_val;
    }
}
```

RMI Limitations

RMI tries hard to hide the complexities of network communication from you. Before you can design a complex application using RMI, however, you have to come to terms with some limitations it imposes on you. In my experience, I have encountered two major limitations in addition to a design concern.

The first limitation springs from the fact that a single line of communication exists between a client and server for each remote object. Figure 8-2 shows the chain of events triggered by a change in an observable object.

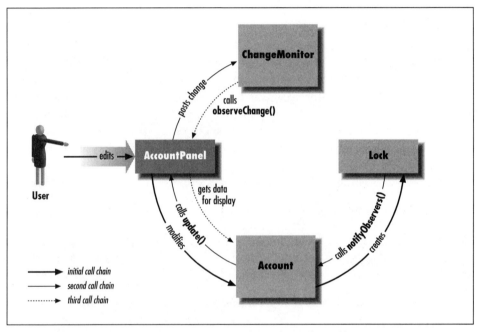

Figure 8-2. The call chain for an observer noticing a change in its observable

Each `Persistent` instance on the application server has a `LockThread` that monitors it for changes and calls `update()` in any observers on the client. Ideally, the observer on the client would turn around and call methods in the `Persistent` that provide the values it should display. Because there is a single line of communication between the `Persistent` and the `PersistentPanel` that blocks on the initial `update()` call, however, any attempt to call methods in the observed object before returning from `update()` will result in a hung system. This is the reason the banking application has the `ChangeMonitor` class.

The solution I have used here is to have a `ChangeObserver`, like `Persistent-Panel`, use the `update()` method to post changes with the `ChangeMonitor` class. This class runs in its own independent thread, allowing `update()` to return immediately. In less than a second, the `ChangeMonitor` pulls the change off the stack and tells the `PersistentPanel` to observe that change.

I personally believe the second limitation to be an RMI design flaw because I know of no technical justification for its existence, and it can seriously impede performance. Specifically, the problem is that a skeleton has no way of recognizing an argument being passed to a method as being local to its virtual machine. Take, for example, the following code:

```
RemoteBall ball = server.getBall();
RemoteBat bat = server.getBat();
ball.hit(bat);
```

In this code, I am passing a `Bat` object I got from the server back to the server. Unfortunately, when the server gets that `Bat` reference, it thinks that object is located on another virtual machine. It never realizes that it is really a local object. The worst problem with this design is that you will incur the costs of a remote method call with any calls you make to that object, even if you are making that call on the server. Local calls involving a remote object passed to the server by a client can end up taking significantly longer to execute than if you were calling that method using the real object instance. And there is no way to get the real instance without writing your own code to map stub references to remote objects.

Another impact of this limitation you have already witnessed in the banking code is the inequality of objects with their remote stubs. You cannot use = or even `equals()` to test if a remote object is equal to its stub. You have to test if the return values of `hashCode()` in each of the objects are the same.

While not really a limitation, the final thing you have to keep in mind is that you must pay careful attention to complex inheritance hierarchies so that you do not end up with casting issues down the road. In the banking application, for example, we have a `CheckingAccount` class that extends `Account` that extends `Persistent`. The respective remote interfaces are `RemoteCheckingAccount`, `RemoteAccount`, and `RemotePersistent`. Each of these interfaces needs to extend each other if we want clients to be able to cast between `RemotePersistent` and `RemoteAccount` and so on.

A Fully Distributed Application

RMI is certainly a topic worthy of its own book, not just the single chapter I have given it here. The focus of this book is to use RMI as a tool in a database application distributed across the network. To that end, we need to turn our focus to making the banking application a distributed application. The majority of the objects that will be available remotely are the business objects. We will spend the rest of this chapter covering any special points in supporting the banking application as a distributed system.

The Observer Pattern

All remote objects must at some point extend the `Remote` interface. Any class that extends a non-remote class but needs to be referenced on a remote virtual machine as an instance of that class is out of luck. Our use of the Java observer classes in Chapter 7 is an excellent example of this problem. The `addObserver()` method in the `java.util.Observable` class takes a `java.util.Observer` implementation as its argument. But `java.util.Observer` does not extend `Remote`. Even though `PersistentPanel` on the client is an implementation of `Observer`, we cannot pass it as a reference across virtual machine boundaries cast as an `Observer`. Our only solution is to rebuild the Java observer utilities in distributed format.

The simplest part of the equation is `RemoteObserver` because it is an interface. Example 8-3 provides the code for a `RemoteObserver` interface.

Example 8-3. The RemoteObserver Interface

```
/**
 * Remote interface for observer objects.
 */
package imaginary.util;

import java.rmi.Remote;
import java.rmi.RemoteException;

public interface RemoteObserver extends Remote {
    public abstract void update(RemoteObservable obs, Object arg)
    throws RemoteException;
}
```

The observable class, however, is more complex. We first need to create an interface that extends `Remote`. Example 8-4 shows this code.

Example 8-4. The RemoteObservable Interface

```
/**
 * Remote interface for the Observable class.
 */
package imaginary.util;

import java.io.Serializable;
import java.rmi.Remote;
import java.rmi.RemoteException;
```

Example 8-4. The RemoteObservable Interface (continued)

```java
public interface RemoteObservable extends Remote {
    public abstract void addObserver(RemoteObserver ob) throws
RemoteException;

    public abstract void deleteObserver(RemoteObserver ob)
    throws RemoteException;

    public abstract int countObservers() throws RemoteException;

    public abstract void notifyObservers() throws RemoteException;

    public abstract void notifyObservers(Remote arg)
    throws RemoteException;

    public abstract void notifyObservers(Serializable arg)
    throws RemoteException;

    public abstract boolean hasChanged() throws RemoteException;
}
```

The first thing you should notice is that only a subset of the
`java.util.Observable` methods are represented in this interface. We want to
put in only the remote interface methods that remote objects should be able to
call. All of the other methods are designed to be called only from within the application server virtual machine.

The actual implementation of `Observable` contains the exact same functionality
as the `java.util.Observable` class with one notable exception: where
`java.util.Observable` accepted any `Object` as an argument to `notify-
Observers()`, this remote version can only accept implementations of `Serial-
izable` or `Remote`. This is because its observers are located across the network;
it must be able to pass any argument to the `update()` method of these remote
observers.

How does it work? The class maintains a `Vector` of observers and a flag to indicate its change status. In Chapter 7, I pointed out how you have to call
`setChanged()` in an `Observable` before a call to `notifyObservers()` will
actually work. In this implementation, `Observable` also will not notify observers
of a call to `notifyObservers()` unless the changed flag is true. Example 8-5
shows the full implementation of `RemoteObservable`.

Example 8-5. A Distributed Version of the java.util.Observable Class

```java
/**
 * This class is a distributed version of the standard Java
 * Observable class.  It uses the exact same API as the Java class.
```

Example 8-5. A Distributed Version of the java.util.Observable Class (continued)

```
 * @see java.util.Observable
 */
package imaginary.util;

import java.io.Serializable;
import java.rmi.Remote;
import java.rmi.RemoteException;
import java.rmi.server.UnicastRemoteObject;
import java.util.Vector;

public class Observable extends UnicastRemoteObject
implements RemoteObservable {
    // the object is ready for observer notification
    private boolean changed  = false;
    // the list of RemoteObserver objects observing this object
    private Vector  observers = new Vector();

    /********************** Constructors ********************/
    /**
     * Constructs a new observable.
     */
    public Observable() {
        super();
    }

    /************** Attribute accessor methods *************/
    /**
     * Marks the observable as unchanged.
     */
    protected synchronized void clearChanged() {
        changed = false;
    }

    /**
     * @return true if the observable is flagged as changed
     */
    public synchronized boolean hasChanged() {
        return changed;
    }

    /**
     * Marks the observable as changed.
     */
    protected synchronized void setChanged() {
        changed = true;
    }

    /**
```

Example 8-5. A Distributed Version of the java.util.Observable Class (continued)

```
 * @return the number of observers observing this object
 */
public synchronized int countObservers() {
    return observers.size();
}


/**
 * Adds a RemoteObserver to the list of objects observing this
 * object.
 * @param ob the new RemoteObserver
 */
public synchronized void addObserver(RemoteObserver ob) {
    if( !observers.contains(ob) ) {
        observers.addElement(ob);
    }
}


/**
 * Removes the specified RemoteObserver from the list of
 * objects being observed.
 * @param ob the RemoteObserver to be removed
 */
public synchronized void deleteObserver(RemoteObserver ob) {
    if( observers.contains(ob) ) {
        observers.removeElement(ob);
    }
}


/**
 * Clears out the entire observer list.
 */
public synchronized void deleteObservers() {
    observers = new Vector();
}


/***************** Observer notification ****************/
/**
 * Assuming the object has been changed, this method
 * will notify its observers with null as an argument.
 */
public void notifyObservers() {
    performNotify(null);
}


/**
 * This method calls performNotify() which calls update()
 * in all observers with the specified remote argument as
 * a parameter.
```

Example 8-5. A Distributed Version of the java.util.Observable Class (continued)

```java
     * @param r the remote object to pass to observers
     */
    public void notifyObservers(Remote r) {
        performNotify(r);
    }

    /**
     * This method calls performNotify() which calls update()
     * in all observers with the specified serializable argument as
     * a parameter.
     * @param s the serializable object to send to the observers
     */
    public void notifyObservers(Serializable s) {
        performNotify(s);
    }

    // This performs actual observer notification.
    // It first copies the observers Vector into an array.
    // This allows it to move out of the synchronized block
    // to avoid dead locks and avoid holding up other threads
    // while it notifies observers across potentially nasty Internet
    // links.  For example, if you synchronized the whole block,
    // processing could take several seconds while some calls time
    // out.  This means another thread coming in and adding to
    // the observer list would wait for this block to release its
    // monitor.  Yuck!
    public void performNotify(Object arg) {
        RemoteObserver[] obs;
        int count;

        synchronized (this) {
            if( !hasChanged() ) {
                return;
            }
            count = observers.size();
            obs = new RemoteObserver[count];
            observers.copyInto(obs);
            clearChanged();
        }
        for(int i=0; i<count; i++) {
            if( obs[i] != null ) {
                try {
                    obs[i].update(this, arg);
                }
                catch( RemoteException e ) {
                    e.printStackTrace();
                }
            }
        }
```

Example 8-5. A Distributed Version of the java.util.Observable Class (continued)

```
        }
    }
}
```

The Persistence Library

We are going to take this new version of the observable pattern and apply it to the persistence library from Chapter 6. When building a complex distributed application, you want to minimize the number of classes you are referencing across virtual machines. Besides the obvious fact that you have to write an interface for each object you distribute, each object also adds complexity to your object model and your application. Added complexity means added chances for problems. For this reason, I am limiting the distribution of persistence library classes to those that absolutely need to be referenced across virtual machines; `Persistent`, `PersistentSet`, and `Lock`. The persistence library also provides a remote interface for a `RemoteLockHolder`, which is subclassed by the client application.

In order to make `Persistent`, `PersistentSet`, and `Lock` remote, we need to provide them with the interfaces `RemotePersistent`, `RemotePersistentSet`, and `RemoteLock`. Example 8-6 provides the `RemotePersistent` interface.

Example 8-6. The RemotePersistent Interface

```
package imaginary.persist;
/**
 * The remote interface for a persistent object.
 */
package imaginary.persist;

import imaginary.util.RemoteObservable;
import java.rmi.RemoteException;

public interface RemotePersistent extends RemoteObservable {
    public abstract boolean isDeleted() throws RemoteException;

    public abstract boolean isLocked() throws RemoteException;

    public abstract boolean isModified() throws RemoteException;

    public abstract boolean isNew() throws RemoteException;

    public abstract boolean isSaving() throws RemoteException;

    public abstract int getId() throws RemoteException;
```

Example 8-6. The RemotePersistent Interface (continued)

```
    public abstract void setNew() throws RemoteException;

    public abstract void remove(RemoteLockHolder h)
    throws LockException, RemoteException;
}
```

Changing the implementations just involves changing any references to objects that will be located on the client to refer to their remote interfaces. Since we always referred to `RemoteLockHolder` by the interface name, there is not a lot we need to change. In fact, the only real change from what we have seen so far is in `PersistentSet`. We need to change `getPersistents()` to return `RemotePeersistent[]` instead of `Persistent[]`. Example 8-7 shows the distributed version of this method.

Example 8-7. The getPersistents() Method from PersistentSet.java

```
public synchronized RemotePersistent[] getPersistents() {
    RemotePersistent[] persistents = new RemotePersistent[objects.size()];

    objects.copyInto(persistents);
    return persistents;
}
```

The Business Objects

Most of the business objects in the application server should be exported to clients; after all, the application server exists to serve these objects to the world. In particular, we need to add remote support to these classes:

- `Customer`
- `CustomerSet`
- `Account`
- `AccountSet`
- `CheckingAccount`
- `SavingsAccount`

We will skip over the `Customer`, `CustomerSet`, and `AccountSet` classes since exporting them is no different from the other classes we have seen in this chapter. The account support, however, is important to understand because it introduces a problem with casting among classes.

In the application server, we instantiate either `CheckingAccount` or `SavingsAccount` objects depending on the account type we find in the database. The client, however, refers to them sometimes as `Account` objects and

other times as their real class. As we distribute the application, the client will
instead refer to those objects as RemoteAccount, RemoteCheckingAccount,
or RemoteSavingsAccount objects. It is really important to be able to cast
among those classes; we have already seen this to a lesser degree in Persistent
(where it needs to be cast to an Observable) and a couple of other places. To
make sure we can do this, we build a parallel line of inheritance between the
interfaces and their implementations. RemoteCheckingAccount extends
RemoteAccount, which extends RemotePersistent, which extends Remote-
Observable, which extends Remote.

Why am I making a big deal out of this? When I was first learning RMI I made the
mistake in a similar situation where instead of having the equivalent of
RemoteCheckingAccount extending RemoteAccount, I simply had CheckingAccount implementing RemoteCheckingAccount and Account
implementing RemoteAccount. This of course compiled and ran through rmic
with flying colors. When I actually had to cast between RemoteCheckingAccount and RemoteAccount on the client, however, I naturally got a
ClassCastException since there was no relationship between those two
classes. If one is an extension of the other, however, then you can cast between
them without trouble.

The Client

One thing that might be bothering you at this point is how the client can pass
remote objects to the server, especially given that it does not run rmiregistry.
RMI allows a bi-directional exchange of objects between client and server so that
an object server can get remote objects served by any client that connects to it; the
client does not need to act as a full-fledged object server. We therefore do not
need to do anything interesting on the client other than look up an instance of
AppServer from the application server. Example 8-8 shows the source code for
the entry class to the client application (which also doubles as the main Frame
class).

Example 8-8. BankClient.java

```
/**
 * BankClient is the main class for the client application.
 * It is invoked by the command line:
 * <PRE>java bank.client.BankClient APP_SERVER_ADDR</PRE>
 * For example:
 * <PRE>java bank.client.BankClient byzantium.imaginary.com</PRE>
 * This class is a subclass of Frame.  At the start of the
 * application, it creates an instance of itself and shows
 * itself, thus starting the application.
 */
```

Example 8-8. BankClient.java (continued)

```java
package bank.client;

import bank.server.RemoteAccount;
import bank.server.RemoteAppServer;
import bank.server.RemoteCustomer;
import imaginary.persist.PersistenceException;
import imaginary.persist.RemoteLock;
import imaginary.persist.RemoteLockHolder;
import imaginary.persist.RemotePersistent;
import java.awt.Button;
import java.awt.Color;
import java.awt.Frame;
import java.awt.Menu;
import java.awt.MenuBar;
import java.awt.MenuItem;
import java.awt.event.ActionEvent;
import java.awt.event.ActionListener;
import java.awt.event.WindowEvent;
import java.awt.event.WindowListener;
import java.rmi.Naming;
import java.rmi.RemoteException;
import java.rmi.server.UnicastRemoteObject;

public class BankClient extends Frame implements RemoteLockHolder,
ActionListener, Runnable, WindowListener {
    static private String host = null;

    /**
     * Sets the static host variable to the first command line
     * argument.  It then creates a new BankClient frame and
     * shows it.
     * @param args the command line arguments to the application
     */
    static public void main(String args[]) {
        try {
            BankClient frame;

            if( args.length != 1 ) {
                System.out.println("Syntax: <java bank.client.BankClient " +
                                "APP_SERVER_HOST>");
                return;
            }
            host = args[0];
            frame =  new BankClient();
            frame.show();
        }
        catch( RemoteException e ) {
            e.printStackTrace();
```

Example 8-8. BankClient.java (continued)

```java
            System.exit(-1);
        }
    }


    private CustomerPanel    customer_panel = null;
    private Menu             account_menu   = null;
    private Menu             help_menu      = null;
    // The lock this RemoteLockHolder holds
    private RemoteLock       lock           = null;
    private MenuBar          menu_bar       = null;
    // The remote application server
    private RemoteAppServer server          = null;


    /**
     * Creates a new instance of this frame object.  Its first
     * task is to export itself as a remote object.  Before
     * it starts to paint itself, it creates a thread
     * in which it connects to the application server.
     * This prevents any network lag from slowing the
     * painting of the screen.
     * @exception java.rmi.RemoteException thrown if the export fails
     */
    public BankClient() throws RemoteException {
        super();
        UnicastRemoteObject.exportObject(this);
        { // Connect to the server in another thread
            Thread t = new Thread(this);

            t.start();
        }
        setTitle("First Imaginary Bank of Java");
        addNotify();
        resize(insets().left + insets().right + 450,insets().top +
                insets().bottom + 256);
        setBackground(new Color(12632256));
        { // Menus
            MenuItem item;

            menu_bar = new MenuBar();
            account_menu = new Menu("Account");
            item = new MenuItem("Open...");
            item.addActionListener(this);
            account_menu.add(item);
            item = new MenuItem("Transfer...");
            item.addActionListener(this);
            account_menu.add(item);
            account_menu.addSeparator();
            item = new MenuItem("Exit");
```

Example 8-8. BankClient.java (continued)

```
            item.addActionListener(this);
            account_menu.add(item);
            menu_bar.add(account_menu);

            help_menu = new Menu("Help");
            menu_bar.setHelpMenu(help_menu);
            item = new MenuItem("About");
            item.addActionListener(this);
            help_menu.add(item);
            menu_bar.add(help_menu);
            setMenuBar(menu_bar);
        }
        customer_panel = new CustomerPanel(this);
        add(customer_panel);
        addWindowListener(this);
        customer_panel.show();
    }


    /**
     * This method runs in a separate thread at the time the
     * frame is created so that it can load the application
     * server.
     */
    public void run() {
        try {
            System.out.println("Connecting to app server at " + host +
                                "...");
            server = (RemoteAppServer)Naming.lookup("rmi://" + host +
                                                "/AppServer");
            System.out.println("Connected to server...");
        }
        catch( Exception e ) {
            System.err.println("Failed to connect to application server.");
            e.printStackTrace();
            server = null;
        }
    }


    /**
     * This is called by the RemoteLock object when it first
     * gets created.
     * @param l the remote lock object for the RemoteLockHolder
     */
    public void setLock(RemoteLock l) {
        lock = l;
    }
```

Example 8-8. BankClient.java (continued)

```java
/**
 * This is called by the remote lock object from time to
 * time just to check if the network is still up.
 * @param p the Persistent this object holds a lock on
 */
public void monitorLock(RemotePersistent p) {
}


/**
 * Move the frame to the proper place when it is shown.
 */
public synchronized void show() {
    move(50, 50);
    super.show();
}


/**
 * JDK 1.1 AWT method for performing ActionListener
 * related functionality.  Specifically, this means responding
 * to menu clicks and button clicks.
 * @param event the triggered event
 */
public void actionPerformed(ActionEvent event) {
    MenuItem m = (MenuItem)event.getSource();
    String l = m.getLabel();

    if( l.equalsIgnoreCase("Open...") ) {
        // Opens a dialog box that prompts the user for a
        // customer ID to open.
        OpenAccountDialog d = new OpenAccountDialog(this, true);

        d.show();
    }
    else if( l.equalsIgnoreCase("Transfer...") ) {
        // Opens a dialog box that allowed a user to
        // specify an amount and target account for
        // money transfers.
        RemoteAccount acct;
        TransferDialog d;

        acct = customer_panel.getSelectedAccount();
        d = new TransferDialog(this, true, acct);
        d.show();
    }
    else if( l.equalsIgnoreCase("About") ) {
        // Shows a simple about dialog
        AboutDialog d = new AboutDialog(this, true);
```

Example 8-8. BankClient.java (continued)

```
            d.show();
        }
        else if( l.equalsIgnoreCase("Exit") ) {
            // Confirms the quit for the user
            QuitDialog d = new QuitDialog(this, true);

            d.show();
        }
    }


    /**
     * The OpenAccountDialog calls this method once the
     * user has entered a customer ID and clicked OK.
     * This method then uses that ID to load a customer
     * object from the application server.
     * @param cust_id the customer ID to be loaded
     */
    public void loadCustomer(int cust_id) {
        RemoteCustomer c;

        try {
            c = server.getCustomer(this, cust_id);
            customer_panel.cleanUp();
            remove(customer_panel);
            customer_panel = new CustomerPanel(this, c);
            add(customer_panel);
            validateTree();
            customer_panel.show();
        }
        catch( PersistenceException e ) {
            System.err.println("Error loading remote customer.");
            e.printStackTrace();
        }
        catch( RemoteException e ) {
            System.err.println("Failed to load remote customer.");
            e.printStackTrace();
        }
    }


    /**
     * The TransferDialog box calls this method with the desired
     * transfer amount, source account, and target account.  The method
     * in turn tells the source account to transfer the specified
     * amount to the specified target account.
     * @param amount the amount of money to transfer
     * @param source the source bank account from which to
     * transfer the funds
```

Example 8-8. BankClient.java (continued)

```java
     * @param target the bank account to which the money will be
transferred
     */
    public synchronized void transfer(float amount, RemoteAccount source,
                                      RemoteAccount target) {
        try {
            source.transfer(this, amount, target);
            lock.save();
        }
        catch( Exception e ) {
            e.printStackTrace();
        }
    }


    // The following methods are required by the WindowListener
    // interface from the JDK 1.1 AWT.
    public void windowActivated(WindowEvent event) {
    }

    public void windowClosed(WindowEvent event) {
    }

    public void windowClosing(WindowEvent event) {
        customer_panel.cleanUp();
        dispose();
        System.exit(0);
    }

    public void windowDeactivated(WindowEvent event) {
    }

    public void windowDeiconified(WindowEvent event) {
    }

    public void windowIconified(WindowEvent event) {
    }

    public void windowOpened(WindowEvent event) {
    }
}
```

We now have a fully distributed client/server application that uses a database for
persistence. We can move it between database engines that have the same tables
without changing any code. In fact, we could even move to file-based persistence
by writing three more classes for the persistence library—SerialTransaction,
SerialPeer, and SerialPeerSet—and implementing the peers for each of
our business objects. I have pointed out several times that this library is not neces-

sarily the most efficient or robust architecture for providing Java object persistence. Nevertheless, over the course of this book, it has hopefully provided you with a solid understanding of JDBC and RMI as well as how to use those technologies in a complex framework.

II

REFERENCE

Chapters 9 and 10 summarize, in a style like *Java in a Nutshell*, the classes you will need to use from the JDBC and RMI APIs.

9

The JDBC API

The `java.sql` package contains the entire JDBC API. It first became part of the core Java libraries with the 1.1 release. Figure 9-1 shows the entire `java.sql` package.

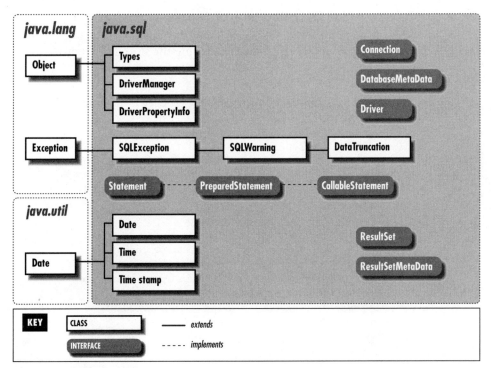

Figure 9-1. The java.sql package

CallableStatement

Synopsis

Class Name:	`java.sql.CallableStatement`
Superclass:	`java.sql.PreparedStatement`
Immediate Subclasses:	None
Interfaces Implemented:	None
Availability:	New as of JDK 1.1

Description

The CallableStatement is an extension of the PreparedStatement interface that provides support for SQL stored procedures. It specifies methods that handle the binding of output parameters. JDBC prescribes a standard form in which stored procedures should appear independent of the DBMS being used. The format is:

```
{? = call …}
{call …}
```

Each question mark is a place holder for an input or output parameter. The first syntax provides for a single result parameter. The second syntax has no result parameters. The parameters are referred to sequentially with the first question mark holding the place for parameter 1.

Before executing a stored procedure, all output parameters should be registered using the `registerOutParameter()` method. You then bind the input parameters using the various set methods, and then execute the stored procedure.

Class Summary

```
public interface CallableStatement extends PreparedStatement {
    // Class Methods
    public abstract String getString(int parameterIndex)
            throws SQLException;
    public abstract BigDecimal getBigDecimal(int parameterIndex,
            int scale) throws SQLException;
    public abstract boolean getBoolean(int parameterIndex)
            throws SQLException;
    public abstract byte getByte(int parameterIndex)
            throws SQLException;
    public abstract byte[] getBytes(int parameterIndex)
            throws SQLException;
    public abstract java.sql.Date getDate(int parameterIndex)
            throws SQLException;
    public abstract double getDouble(int parameterIndex)
            throws SQLException;
    public abstract float getFloat(int parameterIndex)
            throws SQLException;
```

CallableStatement *(continued)*

```
public abstract int getInt(int parameterIndex) throws SQLException;
public abstract long getLong(int parameterIndex)
        throws SQLException;
public abstract Object getObject(int parameterIndex)
        throws SQLException;
public abstract short getShort(int parameterIndex)
        throws SQLException;
public abstract java.sql.Time getTime(int parameterIndex)
        throws SQLException;
public abstract java.sql.Timestamp getTimestamp(int parameterIndex)
        throws SQLException;
public abstract void registerOutParameter(int parameterIndex,
        int sqlType) throws SQLException;
public abstract void registerOutParameter(int parameterIndex,
        int sqlType, int scale) throws SQLException;
public abstract boolean wasNull() throws SQLException;
}
```

Class Methods

getBigDecimal()

```
public abstract BigDecimal getBigDecimal(int parameterIndex, int scale)
        throws SQLException
```

Description

Returns the value of the parameter specified by the parameterIndex parameter as a Java BigDecimal with a scale specified by the scale argument. The scale is a non-negative number representing the number of digits to the right of the decimal. Parameter indices start at 1; parameter 1 is thus parameterIndex 1.

getBoolean(), getBytes(), getDate(), getDouble(), getFloat(), getInt(), getLong(), getString(), getTime(), and getTimestamp()

```
public abstract boolean getBoolean(int parameterIndex)
        throws SQLException
public abstract byte[] getBytes(int parameterIndex) throws SQLException
public abstract Date getDate(int parameterIndex) throws SQLException
public abstract double getDouble(int parameterIndex)
        throws SQLException
public abstract float getFloat(int parameterIndex) throws SQLException
public abstract int getInt(int parameterIndex) throws SQLException
public abstract long getLong(int parameterIndex) throws SQLException
public abstract String getString(int parameterIndex)
        throws SQLException
public abstract Time getTime(int parameterIndex) throws SQLException
```

CallableStatement *(continued)*

```
public abstract Timestamp getTimestamp(int parameterIndex)
      throws SQLException
```

Description

Returns the value of the parameter specified by the `parameterIndex` argument as the Java data type indicated by the method name.

getObject()

```
public abstract Object getObject(int parameterIndex)
      throws SQLException
```
Description

Like the other `getXXX()` methods, this method returns the value of the specified output parameter. In the case of `getObject()`, however, the JDBC driver chooses the Java class that corresponds to the SQL type registered for this parameter using `registerOutParameter()`.

registerOutParameter()

```
public abstract void registerOutParameter(int parameterIndex,
      int sqlType) throws SQLException
public abstract void registerOutParameter(int parameterIndex,
      int sqlType, int scale) throws SQLException
```

Description

Before executing any stored procedure using a `CallableStatement`, you must register each of the output parameters. This method registers the `java.sql.Type` of an output parameter for a stored procedure. The first parameter specifies the output parameter being registered and the second the `java.sql.Type` to register. The three-argument version of this method is for `BigDecimal` types that require a scale. You later read the output parameters using the corresponding `getXXX()` method or `getObject()`.

wasNull()

```
public abstract boolean wasNull() throws SQLException
```

Description

If the last value you read using a `getXXX()` call was SQL NULL, this method will return `true`.

Connection

Synopsis

Class Name:	`java.sql.Connection`
Superclass:	None
Immediate Subclasses:	None
Interfaces Implemented:	None
Availability:	New as of JDK 1.1

Description

The `Connection` class is the JDBC representation of a database session. It provides an application with `Statement` objects (and its subclasses) for that session. It also handles the transaction management for those statements. By default, each statement is committed immediately upon execution. You can use the `Connection` object to turn off this auto-commit feature for the session. In that event, you must expressly send commits, or any statements executed will be lost.

Class Summary

```
public interface Connection {
    static public final int TRANSACTION_NONE;
    static public final int TRANSACTION_READ_UNCOMMITTED;
    static public final int TRANSACTION_READ_COMMITTED;
    static public final int TRANSACTION_REPEATABLE_READ;
    static public final int TRANSACTION_SERIALIZABLE;
    // Class Methods
    public abstract void clearWarnings() throws SQLException;
    public abstract void close() throws SQLException;
    public abstract void commit() throws SQLException;
    public abstract Statement createStatement() throws SQLException;
    public abstract boolean getAutoCommit() throws SQLException;
    public abstract String getCatalog() throws SQLException;
    public abstract int getTransactionIsolation() throws SQLException;
    public abstract SQLWarning getWarnings() throws SQLException;
    public abstract boolean isClosed() throws SQLException;
    public abstract boolean isReadOnly() throws SQLException;
    public abstract DatabaseMetaData getMetaData() throws SQLException;
    public abstract String nativeSQL(String sql) throws SQLException;
    public abstract CallableStatement prepareCall(String sql)
            throws SQLException;
    public abstract PreparedStatement prepareStatement(String sql)
            throws SQLException;
    public abstract void rollback() throws SQLException;
    public abstract void setAutoCommit(boolean autoCommit)
            throws SQLException;
```

Connection *(continued)*

```
public abstract void setCatalog(String catalog)
        throws SQLException;
public abstract void setReadOnly(boolean readOnly)
        throws SQLException;
public abstract void setTransactionIsolation(int level)
        throws SQLException;
}
```

Class Methods

clearWarnings()

```
public abstract void clearWarnings() throws SQLException
```

Description

Clears out all the warnings associated with this Connection so that getWarnings() will return null until a new warning is reported.

close()

```
public abstract void close() throws SQLException
```

Description

This method manually releases all resources (such as network connections and database locks) associated with a given JDBC Connection. This method is automatically called when garbage collection occurs; however, it is best to manually close a Connection once you are done with it.

commit()

```
public abstract void commit() throws SQLException
```

Description

This method makes permanent the changes created by all statements associated with this Connection since the last commit or rollback was issued. It should only be used when auto-commit is off. It does not commit changes made by statements associated with other Connection objects.

createStatement()

```
public abstract Statement createStatement() throws SQLException
```

Description

This method creates a Statement object associated with this Connection session.

Connection (continued)

getAutoCommit() and setAutoCommit()

```
public abstract boolean getAutoCommit() throws SQLException
public abstract void setAutoCommit(boolean autoCommit)
     throws SQLException
```

Description

By default, all Connection objects are in auto-commit mode. With auto-commit mode on, each statement is committed as it is executed. An application may instead choose to manually commit a series of statements together as a single transaction. In this case, you use the setAuto-Commit() method to turn auto-commit off. You then follow your statements with a call to commit() or rollback() depending on the success or failure of the transaction.

When in auto-commit mode, a statement is committed either when the statement completes or when the next statement is executed, whichever is first. For statements returning a ResultSet, the statement completes when the last row has been retrieved or the ResultSet has been closed. If a statement returns multiple result sets, the commit occurs when the last row of the last ResultSet object has been retrieved.

getCatalog() and setCatalog()

```
public abstract String getCatalog() throws SQLException
public abstract void setCatalog(String catalog) throws SQLException
```

Description

If a driver supports catalogs, then you use setCatalog() to select a subspace of the database with the specified catalog name. If the driver does not support catalogs, it will ignore this request.

getMetaData()

```
public abstract DatabaseMetaData getMetaData() throws SQLException
```

Description

The DatabaseMetaData class provides methods that describe a database's tables, SQL support, stored procedures, and other information relating to the database and this Connection that are not directly related to executing statements and retrieving result sets. This method provides an instance of the DatabaseMetaData class for this Connection.

getTransactionIsolation() and setTransactionIsolation()

```
public abstract int getTransactionIsolation() throws SQLException
public abstract void setTransactionIsolation(int level)
     throws SQLException
```

Connection (continued)

Description

Sets the Connection object's current transaction isolation level using one of the class attributes for the `Connection` interface. Those levels are called `TRANSACTION_NONE`, `TRANSACTION_READ_UNCOMMITTED`, `TRANSACTION_READ_COMMITTED`, and `TRANSACTION_REPEATABLE_READ`.

getWarnings()

```
public abstract SQLWarning getWarnings() throws SQLException
```

Description

Returns the first warning in the chain of warnings associated with this `Connection` object.

isClosed()

```
public abstract boolean isClosed() throws SQLException
```

Description

Returns `true` if the Connection has been closed.

isReadOnly() and setReadOnly()

```
public abstract boolean isReadOnly() throws SQLException
public abstract void setReadOnly(boolean readOnly) throws SQLException
```

Description

Some databases can optimize for read-only database access. The `setReadOnly()` method provides you with a way to put a `Connection` into read-only mode so that those optimizations occur. You cannot call `setReadOnly()` while in the middle of a transaction.

nativeSQL()

```
public abstract String nativeSQL(String sql) throws SQLException
```

Description

Many databases may not actually support the same SQL required by JDBC. This method allows an application to see the native SQL for a given JDBC SQL string.

prepareCall()

```
public abstract CallableStatement prepareCall(String sql)
    throws SQLException
```

Connection (continued)

Description

Given a particular SQL string, this method creates a `CallableState-`
`ment` object associated with this `Connection` session. This is the
preferred way of handling stored procedures.

prepareStatement()

```
public abstract PreparedStatement prepareStatement(String sql)
    throws SQLException
```

Description

Provides a `PreparedStatement` object to be associated with this
`Connection` session. This is the preferred way of handling precompiled
SQL statements.

rollback()

```
public abstract void rollback() throws SQLException
```

Description

Aborts all changes made by statements associated with this Connection
since the last time a commit or rollback was issued. If you want to make
those changes at a later time, your application will have to re-execute the
statements that made those changes. This should be used only when auto-
commit is off.

DatabaseMetaData

Synopsis

Class Name:	`java.sql.DatabaseMetaData`
Superclass:	None
Immediate Subclasses:	None
Interfaces Implemented:	None
Availability:	New as of JDK 1.1

Description

This class provides a lot of information about the database to which a `Connec-`
`tion` object is connected. In many cases, it returns this information in the form
of JDBC `ResultSet` objects. For databases that do not support a particular kind
of metadata, `DatabaseMetaData` will throw an SQLException.

DatabaseMetaData *(continued)*

DatabaseMetaData methods take string patterns as arguments where specific tokens within the String are interpreted to have a certain meaning. % matches any substring of 0 or more characters and _ matches any one character. You can pass null to methods in place of string pattern arguments; this means that the argument's criteria should be dropped from the search.

The DatabaseMetaData class consists of 130+ methods relating mostly to obscure information about the database being used. I have therefore decided to leave out detailed descriptions of them to save on what would mostly be wasted space.

Class Summary

```
public interface DatabaseMetaData {
    static public final int bestRowTemporary;
    static public final int bestRowTransaction;
    static public final int bestRowSession;
    static public final int bestRowUnknown;
    static public final int bestRowNotPseudo;
    static public final int bestRowPseudo;
    static public final int columnNoNulls;
    static public final int columnNullable;
    static public final int columnNullableUnknown;
    static public final int importedKeyCascade;
    static public final int importedKeyRestrict;
    static public final int importedKeySetNull;
    static public final int importedKeyNoAction;
    static public final int importedKeySetDefault;
    static public final int importedKeyInitiallyDeferred;
    static public final int importedKeyInitiallyImmediate;
    static public final int importedKeyNotDeferrable;
    static public final int procedureResultUnknown;
    static public final int procedureNoResult;
    static public final int procedureReturnsResult;
    static public final int procedureColumnUnknown;
    static public final int procedureColumnIn;
    static public final int procedureColumnOut;
    static public final int procedureColumnReturn;
    static public final int procedureColumnResult;
    static public final int procedureNoNulls;
    static public final int procedureNullable;
    static public final int procedureNullableUnknown;
    static public final short tableIndexStatistic;
    static public final short tableIndexClustered;
    static public final short tableIndexHashed;
    static public final short tableIndexOther;
```

DatabaseMetaData (continued)

```
static public final int typeNoNulls;
static public final int typeNullable;
static public final int typeNullableUnknown;
static public final int typePredNone;
static public final int typePredChar;
static public final int typePredBasic;
static public final int typeSearchable;
static public final int versionColumnUnknown;
static public final int versionColumnNotPseudo;
static public final int versionColumnPseudo;
// Class Methods
public abstract boolean allProceduresAreCallable()
        throws SQLException;
public abstract boolean allTablesAreSelectable()
        throws SQLException;
public abstract boolean dataDefinitionCausesTransactionCommit()
        throws SQLException;
public abstract boolean dataDefinitionIgnoredInTransactions()
        throws SQLException;
public abstract ResultSet getBestRowIdentifier(String catalog,
        String schema, String table, int scope, boolean nullable)
        throws SQLException;
public abstract ResultSet getCatalogs() throws SQLException;
public abstract String getCatalogSeparator() throws SQLException;
public abstract String getCatalogTerm() throws SQLException;
public abstract ResultSet getColumnPriveleges(String catalog,
        String schemaPattern, String table,
        String columnNamePattern) throws SQLException;
public abstract ResultSet getColumns(String catalog,
        String schemaPattern, String tableNamePattern,
        String columnNamePattern) throws SQLException;
public abstract ResultSet getCrossReference(String primaryCatalog,
        String primarySchema, String primaryTable,
        String foreignCatalog, String foreignSchema,
        String foreignTable) throws SQLException;
public abstract String getDatabaseProductName()
        throws SQLException;
public abstract String getDatabaseProductVersion()
        throws SQLException;
public abstract int getDefaultTransactionIsolation()
        throws SQLException;
public abstract int getDriverMajorVersion();
public abstract int getDriverMinorVersion();
public abstract String getDriverName() throws SQLException;
public abstract String getDriverVersion() throws SQLException;
public abstract resultSet getExportedKeys(String catalog,
        String schema, String table) throws SQLException;
```

DatabaseMetaData *(continued)*

```
public abstract String getExtraNameCharacters()
        throws SQLException;
public abstract String getIdentifierQuoteString()
        throws SQLException;
public abstract ResultSet getImportedKeys(String catalog,
        String schema, String table) throws SQLException;
public abstract ResultSet getIndexInfo(String catalog,
        String schema, String table, boolean unique,
        boolean approximate) throws SQLException;
public abstract int getMaxBinaryLiteralLength()
        throws SQLException;
public abstract int getMaxCatalogNameLength() throws SQLException;
public abstract int getMaxCharLiteralLength() throws SQLException;
public abstract int getMaxColumnNameLength() throws SQLException;
public abstract int getMaxColumnsInGroupBy() throws SQLException;
public abstract int getMaxColumnsInIndex() throws SQLException;
public abstract int getMaxColumnsInOrderBy() throws SQLException;
public abstract int getMaxColumnsInSelect() throws SQLException;
public abstract int getMaxColumnsInTable() throws SQLException;
public abstract int getMaxConnections() throws SQLException;
public abstract int getMaxIndexLength() throws SQLException;
public abstract int getMaxProcedureNameLength()
        throws SQLException;
public abstract int getMaxRowSize() throws SQLException;
public abstract int getMaxRowSizeIncludeBlobs()
        throws SQLException;
public abstract int getMaxSchemaNameLength() throws SQLException;
public abstract int getMaxStatementLength() throws SQLException;
public abstract int getMaxStatements() throws SQLException;
public abstract int getMaxTableNameLength() throws SQLException;
public abstract int getMaxTablesInSelect() throws SQLException;
public abstract int getMaxUserNameLength() throws SQLException;
public abstract String getNumericFunctions() throws SQLException;
public abstract ResultSet getPrimaryKeys(String catalog,
        String schema, String table) throws SQLException;
public abstract ResultSet getProcedureColumns(String catalog,
        String schemePattern, String procedureNamePattern,
        String columnNamePattern) throws SQLException;
public abstract String getProcedureTerm() throws SQLException;
public abstract ResultSet getProcedures(String catalog,
        String schemaPattern, String procedureNamePattern)
        throws SQLException;
public abstract ResultSet getSchemas() throws SQLException;
public abstract String getSchemaTerm() throws SQLException;
public abstract String getSearchStringEscape() throws SQLException;
public abstract String getSQLKeywords() throws SQLException;
public abstract String getStringFunctions() throws  SQLException;
```

DatabaseMetaData (continued)

```
public abstract String getSystemFunctions() throws SQLException;
public abstract ResultSet getTablePriveleges(String catalog,
        String schemaPattern, String tableNamePattern)
        throws SQLException;
public abstract ResultSet getTableTypes() throws SQLException;
public abstract ResultSet getTables(String catalog,
        String schemaPattern, String tableNamePattern,
        String types[]) throws SQLException;
public abstract String getTimeDateFunctions() throws SQLException;
public abstract ResultSet getTypeInfo() throws SQLException;
public abstract String getURL() throws SQLException;
public abstract String getUserName() throws SQLException;
public abstract ResultSet getVersionColumns(String catalog,
        String schema, String table) throws SQLException;
public abstract boolean isCatalogAtStart() throws SQLException;
public abstract boolean isReadOnly() throws SQLException;
public abstract boolean nullPlusNonNullIsNull()
        throws SQLException;
public abstract boolean nullsAreSortedHigh() throws SQLException;
public abstract boolean nullsAreSortedLow() throws SQLException;
public abstract boolean nullsAreSortedAtStart()
        throws SQLException;
public abstract boolean nullsAreSortedAtEnd() throws SQLException;
public abstract boolean storesLowerCaseIdentifiers()
        throws SQLException;
public abstract boolean storesLowerCaseQuotedIdentifiers()
        throws SQLException;
public abstract boolean storesMixedCaseIdentifiers()
        throws SQLException;
public abstract boolean storesMixedCaseQuotedIdentifiers()
        throws SQLException;
public abstract boolean storesUpperCaseIdentifiers()
        throws SQLException;
public abstract boolean storesUpperCaseQuotedIdentifiers()
        throws SQLException;
public abstract boolean supportsAlterTableWithAddColumn()
        throws SQLException;
public abstract boolean supportsAlterTableWithDropColumn()
        throws SQLException;
public abstract boolean supportsANSI92FullSQL()
        throws SQLException;
public abstract boolean supportsANSI92IntermediateSQL()
        throws SQLException;
public abstract boolean supportsCatalogsInDataManipulation()
        throws SQLException;
public abstract boolean suppportsCatalogsInIndexDefinitions()
        throws SQLException;
```

DatabaseMetaData (continued)

```
public abstract boolean supportsCatalogsInPrivelegeDefinitions()
        throws SQLException;
public abstract boolean supportsCatalogsInProcedureCalls()
        throws SQLException;
public abstract boolean supportsCatalogsInTableDefinitions()
        throws SQLException;
public abstract boolean supportsColumnAliasing()
        throws SQLException;
public abstract boolean supportsConvert() throws SQLException;
public abstract boolean supportsConvert(int fromType, int toType)
        throws SQLException;
public abstract boolean supportsCoreSQLGrammar()
        throws SQLException;
public abstract boolean supportsCorrelatedSubqueries()
        throws SQLException; public abstract boolean
supportsDataDefinitionAndDataManipulationTransactions()
        throws SQLException;
public abstract boolean supportsDataManipulationTransactionsOnly()
        throws SQLException;
public abstract boolean supportsDifferentTableCorrelationNames()
        throws SQLException;
public abstract boolean supportsExpressionsInOrderBy()
        throws SQLException;
public abstract boolean supportsExtendedSQLGrammar()
        throws SQLException;
public abstract boolean supportsFullOuterJoins()
        throws SQLException;
public abstract boolean supportsGroupBy() throws SQLException;
public abstract boolean supportsGroupByBeyondSelect()
        throws SQLException;
public abstract boolean supportsGroupByUnrelated()
        throws SQLException;
public abstract boolean supportsIntegrityEnhancementFacility()
        throws SQLException;
public abstract boolean supportsLikeEscapeClause()
        throws SQLException;
public abstract boolean supportsLimitedOuterJoins()
        throws SQLException;
public abstract boolean supportsMinimumSQLGrammar()
        throws SQLException;
public abstract boolean supportsMixedCaseIdentifiers()
        throws SQLException;
public abstract boolean supportsMixedCaseQuotedIdenfitiers()
        throws SQLException;
public abstract boolean supportsMultipleResultSets()
        throws SQLException;
```

DatabaseMetaData (continued)

```
public abstract boolean supportsMultipleTransactions()
        throws SQLException;
public abstract boolean supportsNonNullableColumns()
        throws SQLException;
public abstract boolean supportsOpenCursorsAcrossCommit()
        throws SQLException;
public abstract boolean supportsOpenCursorsAcrossRollback()
        throws SQLException;
public abstract boolean supportsOpenStatementsAcrossCommit()
        throws SQLException;
public abstract boolean supportsOpenStatementsAcrossRollback()
        throws SQLException;
public abstract boolean supportsOrderByUnrelated()
        throws SQLException;
public abstract boolean supportsOuterJoins() throws SQLException;
public abstract boolean supportsPositionedDelete()
        throws SQLException;
public abstract boolean supportsPositionedUpdate()
        throws SQLException;
public abstract boolean supportsSchemasInDataManipulation()
        throws SQLException;
public abstract boolean supportsSchemasInIndexDefinitions()
        throws SQLException;
public abstract boolean supportsSchemasInPrivelegeDefinitions()
        throws SQLException;
public abstract boolean supportsSchemasInProcedureCalls()
        throws SQLException;
public abstract boolean supportsSchemasInTableDefinitions()
        throws SQLException;
public abstract boolean supportsSelectForUpdate()
        throws SQLException;
public abstract boolean supportsStoredProcedures()
        throws SQLException;
public abstract boolean supportsSubqueriesInComparisons()
        throws SQLException;
public abstract boolean supportsSubqueriesInExists()
        throws SQLException;
public abstract boolean supportsSubqueriesInIns()
        throws SQLException;
public abstract boolean supportsSubqueriesInQuantifieds()
        throws SQLException;
public abstract boolean supportsTableCorrelationNames()
        throws SQLException;
public boolean supportsTransactionIsolationLevel(int level)
        throws SQLException;
public abstract boolean supportsTransactions() throws SQLException;
public abstract boolean supportsUnion() throws SQLException;
```

DatabaseMetaData (continued)

```
    public abstract boolean supportsUnionAll() throws SQLException;
    public abstract boolean usesLocalFilePerTable()
            throws SQLException;
    public abstract boolean usesLocalFiles() throws SQLException;
}
```

Date

Synopsis

Class Name:	`java.sql.Date`
Superclass:	`java.util.Date`
Immediate Subclasses:	None
Interfaces Implemented:	None
Availability:	New as of JDK 1.1

Description

This class deals with a subset of functionality found in the `java.util.Date` class. It specifically worries only about days and ignores hours, minutes, and seconds.

Class Summary

```
    public class Date extends java.util.Date {
        // Class Methods
        static public Date valueOf(String s);
        public Date(int year, int month, int day);
        public String toString();
    }
```

Class Methods

Date()

```
    public Date(int year, int month, int day)
```

Description

Constructs a date corresponding with the year, month, and day specified.

toString()

```
    public String toString()
```

Description

Provides a `String` representing this `Date` in the form `yyyy-mm-dd`.

Date (*continued*)

valueOf()

```
static public Date valueOf(String s)
```

Description

> Given a String in the form of yyyy-mm-dd, this will return a corresponding instance of the Date class representing that date.

Driver

Synopsis

Class Name: java.sql.Driver
Superclass: None
Immediate Subclasses: None
Interfaces Implemented: None
Availability: New as of JDK 1.1

Description

This class represents a specific JDBC implementation. When a Driver is loaded, it should create an instance of itself and register that instance with the Driver-Manager class. This allows applications to create instances of it using the Class.forName() call to load a driver.

The Driver object then provides the ability for an application to connect to one or more databases. When a request for a specific database comes through, the DriverManager will pass the data source request to each Driver registered as a URL. The first Driver to connect to the data source using that URL will be used.

Class Summary

```
public interface Driver {
    // Class Methods
    public abstract boolean acceptsURL(String url) throws SQLException;
    public abstract Connection connect(String url, Properties info)
            throws SQLException;
    public abstract int getMajorVersion();
    public abstract int getMinorVersion();
    public abstract DriverPropertyInfo[] getPropertyInfo(String url,
            Properties info) throws SQLException;
    public abstract boolean jdbcCompliant();
}
```

Driver *(continued)*

Class Methods

acceptsURL()

```
public abstract boolean acceptsURL(String url) throws SQLException
```

Description

Returns true if the specified URL matches the URL subprotocol used by this driver.

connect()

```
public abstract Connection connect(String url, Properties info)
      throws SQLException
```

Description

This method attempts a connect using the specified URL and Property information (usually containing the user name and password). If the URL is not right for this driver, connect() simply returns null. If it is the right URL, but an error occurs during the connection process, an SQLException should be thrown.

getMajorVersion()

```
public abstract int getMajorVersion()
```

Description

Returns the major version number for the driver.

getMinorVersion()

```
public abstract int getMinorVersion()
```

Description

Returns the minor version number for the driver.

getPropertyInfo()

```
public abstract DriverPropertyInfo[] getPropertyInfo(String url,
      Properties info) throws SQLException;
```

Description

This method allows GUI-based RAD environments to find out which properties the driver needs on connect so that it can prompt a user to enter values for those properties.

jdbcCompliant()

```
public abstract boolean jdbcCompliant()
```

Driver (*continued*)

Description

A Driver can return true here only if it passes the JDBC compliance tests. This means that the driver implementation supports the full JDBC API and full SQL 92 Entry Level.

DriverManager

Synopsis

Class Name:	`java.sql.DriverManager`
Superclass:	`java.lang.Object`
Immediate Subclasses:	None
Interfaces Implemented:	None
Availability:	New as of JDK 1.1

Description

The `DriverManager` holds the master list of registered JDBC drivers for the system. Upon initialization, it loads all classes specified in the `jdbc.drivers` property. You can thus specify any runtime information about the database being used by an application on the command line.

During program execution, other drivers may register themselves with the `DriverManager` by calling the `registerDriver()` method. The `DriverManager` uses a JDBC URL to find an application's desired driver choice when requests are made through `getConnection()`.

Class Summary

```
public class DriverManager {
    // Class Methods
    static public synchronized Connection getConnection(String url,
            Properties info) throws SQLException;
    static public synchronized Connection getConnection(String url,
            String user, String password) throws SQLException;
    static public synchronized Connection getConnection(String url)
            throws SQLException;
    static public Driver getDriver(String url) throws SQLException;
    static public Enumeration getDrivers();
    static public int getLoginTimeout();
    static public PrintStream getLogStream();
    static public void deregisterDriver(Driver driver)
            throws SQLException;
```

DriverManager (continued)

```
static public void println(String message);
static public synchronized void registerDriver(Driver driver)
      throws SQLException;
static public void setLogStream(PrintStream out);
static public void setLoginTimeout(int seconds);
}
```

Class Methods

deregisterDriver()

```
static public void deregisterDriver(Driver driver) throws SQLException
```

Description

Removes a Driver from the list of registered drivers.

getConnection()

```
static public synchronized Connection getConnection(String url,
      Properties info) throws SQLException
static public synchronized Connection getConnection(String url,
      String user, String password) throws SQLException
static public synchronized Connection getConnection(String url)
      throws SQLException
```

Description

Establishes a connection to the data store represented by the URL given. The DriverManager then looks through its list of registered Driver instances for one that will handle the specified URL. If none is found, it throws an SQLException. Otherwise it returns the Connection instance from the connect() method in the Driver class.

getDriver()

```
static public Driver getDriver(String url) throws SQLException
```

Description

Returns a driver than can handle the specified URL.

getDrivers()

```
static public Enumeration getDrivers()
```

Description

Returns a list of all registered drivers.

getLoginTimeout() and setLoginTimeout()

```
static public int getLoginTimeout()
static public int setLoginTimeout()
```

DriverManager (continued)

Description

The login timeout is the maximum time in seconds that a driver can wait in attempting to log in to a database.

getLogStream() and setLogStream()

```
static public PrintStream getLogStream()
static public void setLogStream(PrintStream out)
```

Description

Set and retrieve the PrintStream used for logging for the Driver-Manager and all drivers.

println()

```
static public void println(String message)
```

Description

Prints a message to the current log stream.

registerDriver()

```
static public synchronized void registerDriver(Driver driver)
        throws SQLException
```

Description

This method allows a newly loaded Driver to register itself with the DriverManager class.

DriverPropertyInfo

Synopsis

Class Name:	java.sql.DriverPropertyInfo
Superclass:	java.lang.Object
Immediate Subclasses:	None
Interfaces Implemented:	None
Availability:	New as of JDK 1.1

Description

This class provides information required by a driver in order to connect to a database. Only development tools are likely ever to require this class. It has no methods, simply a list of public attributes.

DriverPropertyInfo (continued)

Class Summary

```
public class DriverPropertyInfo {
    // Class Methods
    public String name;         // property name
    public String description;  // property description
    public boolean required;    // is it required?
    public String value;        // what is the current value?
    public String choices[];
    public DriverPropertyInfo(String name, String value);
}
```

PreparedStatement

Synopsis

Class Name:	java.sql.PreparedStatement
Superclass:	java.sql.Statement
Immediate Subclasses:	java.sql.CallableStatement
Interfaces Implemented:	None
Availability:	New as of JDK 1.1

Description

This class represents a precompiled SQL statement.

Class Summary

```
public interface PreparedStatement extends Statement {
    // Class Methods
    public abstract void clearParameters() throws SQLException;
    public abstract boolean execute() throws SQLException;
    public abstract ResultSet executeQuery() throws SQLException;
    public abstract int executeUpdate() throws SQLException;
    public abstract void setAsciiStream(int parameterIndex,
            InputStream x,
            int length) throws SQLException;
    public abstract void setBigDecimal(int parameterIndex,
            BigDecimal x)
            throws SQLException;
    public abstract void setBinaryStream(int parameterIndex,
            InputStream x,
            int length) throws SQLException;
    public abstract void setBoolean(int parameterIndex, boolean x)
            throws SQLException;
```

PreparedStatement (continued)

```
public abstract void setByte(int parameterIndex, byte x)
        throws SQLException;
public abstract void setBytes(int parameterIndex, byte[] x)
        throws SQLException;
public abstract void setDate(int parameterIndex, Date x)
        throws SQLException;
public abstract void setDouble(int parameterIndex, double x)
        throws SQLException;
public abstract void setFloat(int parameterIndex, float x)
        throws SQLException;
public abstract void setInt(int parameterIndex, int x)
        throws SQLException;
public abstract void setLong(int parameterIndex, long x)
        throws SQLException;
public abstract void setNull(int parameterIndex, int sqlType)
        throws SQLException;
public abstract void setObject(int parameterIndex, Object x)
        throws SQLException;
public abstract void setObject(int parameterIndex,
        int targetSqlType, int scale)
        throws SQLException;
public abstract void setObject(int parameterIndex, Object x,
        int targetSqlType) throws SQLException;
public abstract void setShort(int parameterIndex, short x)
        throws SQLException;
public abstract void setString(int parameterIndex, String x)
        throws SQLException;
public abstract void setTime(int parameterIndex, Time x)
        throws SQLExcepption;
public abstract void setTimestamp(int parameterIndex, Timestamp x)
        throws SQLException;
public abstract void setUnicodeStream(int parameterIndex,
        InputStream x,
        int length) throws SQLException;
}
```

Class Methods

clearParameters()

```
public abstract void clearParameters() throws SQLException
```

Description

Once set, a parameter value remains bound until either a new value is set for the parameter or until `clearParameters()` is called. This method clears all parameters associated with the `PreparedStatement`.

PreparedStatement *(continued)*

execute(), executeQuery(), and executeUpdate()

```
public abstract boolean execute() throws SQLException
public abstract ResultSet executeQuery() throws SQLException
public abstract int executeUpdate() throws SQLException
```

Description

Executes the PreparedStatement. The first method, execute(), allows you to execute the PreparedStatement when you do not know if it is a query or an update. It returns true if the statement has result sets to process.

The executeQuery() method is used for executing queries. It returns a result set for processing.

The executeUpdate() statement is used for executing updates. It returns the number of rows affected by the update.

setAsciiStream(), setBigDecimal(), setBinaryStream(), setBoolean(), setByte(), setBytes(), setDate(), setDouble(), setFloat(), setInt(), setLong(), setNull(), setObject(), setShort(), setString(), setTime(), setTimestamp(), and setUnicodeStream()

```
public abstract void setAsciiStream(int parameterIndex, InputStream x,
        int length) throws SQLException
public abstract void setBigDecimal(int parameterIndex, BigDecimal x)
        throws SQLException
public abstract void setBinaryStream(int parameterIndex, InputStream x,
        int length) throws SQLException
public abstract void setBoolean(int parameterIndex, boolean x)
        throws SQLException
public abstract void setByte(int parameterIndex, byte x)
        throws SQLException
public abstract void setBytes(int parameterIndex, byte[] x)
        throws SQLException
public abstract void setDate(int parameterIndex, Date x)
        throws SQLException
public abstract void setDouble(int parameterIndex, double x)
        throws SQLException
public abstract void setFloat(int parameterIndex, float x)
        throws SQLException
public abstract void setInt(int parameterIndex, int x)
        throws SQLException
public abstract void setLong(int parameterIndex, long x)
        throws SQLException
public abstract void setNull(int parameterIndex, int sqlType)
        throws SQLException
```

PreparedStatement *(continued)*

```
public abstract void setObject(int parameterIndex, Object x)
        throws SQLException
public abstract void setObject(int parameterIndex, int targetSqlType,
        int scale) throws SQLException
public abstract void setObject(int parameterIndex, Object x,
        int targetSqlType) throws SQLException
public abstract void setShort(int parameterIndex, short x)
        throws SQLException
public abstract void setString(int parameterIndex, String x)
        throws SQLException
public abstract void setTime(int parameterIndex, Time x)
        throws SQLException
public abstract void setTimestamp(int parameterIndex, Timestamp x)
        throws SQLException
public abstract void setUnicodeStream(int parameterIndex,
        InputStream x, int length)
        throws SQLException
```

Description

Binds a value to the specified parameter.

ResultSet

Synopsis

Class Name:	`java.sql.ResultSet`
Superclass:	None
Immediate Subclasses:	None
Interfaces Implemented:	None
Availability:	New as of JDK 1.1

Description

This class represents a database result set. It provides an application with access to database queries one row at a time. During query processing, a `ResultSet` maintains a pointer to the current row being manipulated. The application then moves through the results sequentially until all results have been processed or the `ResultSet` is closed. A `ResultSet` is automatically closed when the `State-ment` that generated it is closed, re-executed, or used to retrieve the next `ResultSet` in a multiple result set query.

ResultSet *(continued)*

Class Summary

```
public interface ResultSet {
    // Class Methods
    public abstract void clearWarnings() throws SQLException;
    public abstract void close() throws SQLException;
    public abstract int findColumn(String columnName)
            throws SQLException;
    public abstract InputStream getAsciiStream(int columnIndex)
            throws SQLException;
    public abstract InputStream getAsciiStream(String columnName)
            throws SQLException;
    public abstract InputStream getBinaryStream(int columnIndex)
            throws SQLException;
    public abstract InputStream getBinaryStream(String columnName)
            throws SQLException;
    public abstract BigDecimal getBigDecimal(int columnIndex,
            int scale)
            throws SQLException;
    public abstract BigDecimal getBigDecimal(String columnName,
            int scale)
            throws SQLException;
    public abstract boolean getBoolean(int columnIndex)
            throws SQLException;
    public abstract boolean getBoolean(String columnName)
            throws SQLException;
    public abstract byte getByte(int columnIndex) throws SQLException;
    public abstract byte getByte(String columnName)
            throws SQLException;
    public abstract byte[] getBytes(int columnIndex)
            throws SQLException;
    public abstract byte[] getBytes(String columnName)
            throws SQLException;
    public abstract String getCursorName() throws SQLException;
    public abstract Date getDate(int columnIndex) throws SQLException;
    public abstract Date getDate(String columnName)
            throws SQLException;
    public abstract double getDouble(int columnIndex)
            throws SQLException;
    public abstract double getDouble(String columnName)
            throws SQLException;
    public abstract float getFloat(int columnIndex)
            throws SQLException;
    public abstract float getFloat(String columnName)
            throws SQLException;
    public abstract int getInt(int columnIndex) throws SQLException;
    public abstract int getInt(String columnName) throws SQLException;
```

ResultSet *(continued)*

```
public abstract long getLong(int columnIndex) throws SQLException;
public abstract long getLong(String columnName)
        throws SQLException;
public abstract ResultSetMetaData getMetaData()
        throws SQLException;
public abstract Object getObject(int columnIndex)
        throws SQLException;
public abstract Object getObject(String columnName)
        throws SQLException;
public abstract short getShort(int columnIndex)
        throws SQLException;
public abstract short getShort(String columnName)
        throws SQLException;
public abstract String getString(int columnIndex)
        throws SQLException;
public abstract String getString(String columnName)
        throws SQLException;
public abstract Time getTime(int columnIndex) throws SQLException;
public abstract Time getTime(String columnName)
        throws SQLException;
public abstract Timestamp getTimestamp(int columnIndex)
        throws SQLException;
public abstract Timestamp getTimestamp(String columnName)
        throws SQLException;
public abstract InputStream getUnicodeStream(int columnIndex)
        throws SQLException;
public abstract InputStream getUnicodeStream(String columnName)
        throws SQLException;
public abstract SQLWarning getWarnings() throws SQLException;
public abstract boolean next() throws SQLException;
public abstract boolean wasNull() throws SQLException;
}
```

Class Methods

clearWarnings()

```
public abstract void clearWarnings() throws SQLException
```

Description

Clears all warnings from the SQLWarning chain. Subsequent calls to getWarnings() then returns null until another warning occurs.

close()

```
public abstract void close() throws SQLException
```

ResultSet *(continued)*

Description

> Performs an immediate, manual close of the ResultSet. This is gener-
> ally never required, as the closure of the Statement associated with the
> ResultSet will automatically close the ResultSet.

findColumn()

```
public abstract int findColumn(String columnName) throws SQLException
```

Description

> For the specified column name, this method will return the column
> number associated with it.

getAsciiStream(), getBinaryStream(), and getUnicodeStream()

```
public abstract InputStream getAsciiStream(int columnIndex)
        throws SQLException
public abstract InputStream getAsciiStream(String columnName)
        throws SQLException
public abstract InputStream getBinaryStream(int columnIndex)
        throws SQLException
public abstract InputStream getBinaryStream(String columnName)
        throws SQLException
public abstract InputStream getUnicodeStream(int columnIndex)
        throws SQLException
public abstract InputStream getUnicodeStream(String columnName)
        throws SQLException
```

Description

> In some cases, it may make sense to retrieve large pieces of data from the
> database as a Java InputStream. These methods allow an application to
> retrieve the specified column from the current row in this manner.

getBigDecimal()

```
public abstract BigDecimal getBigDecimal(int columnIndex, int scale)
        throws SQLException
public abstract BigDecimal getBigDecimal(String columnName, int scale)
        throws SQLException
```

Description

> Returns the value of the specified column from the current row as a Java
> BigDecimal object. The scale is a non-negative number representing
> the number of digits to the right of the decimal.

ResultSet *(continued)*

getBoolean(), getByte(), getBytes(), getDate(), getDouble(), getFloat(), getInt(), getLong(), getShort(), getString(), getTime(), and getTimestamp()

```
public abstract boolean getBoolean(int columnIndex) throws SQLException
public abstract boolean getBoolean(String columnName)
        throws SQLException
public abstract byte getByte(int columnIndex) throws SQLException
public abstract byte getByte(String columnName) throws SQLException
public abstract byte[] getBytes(int columnIndex) throws SQLException
public abstract byte[] getBytes(String columnName) throws SQLException
public abstract Date getDate(int columnIndex) throws SQLException
public abstract Date getDate(String columnName) throws SQLException
public abstract double getDouble(int columnIndex) throws SQLException
public abstract double getDouble(String columnName) throws SQLException
public abstract float getFloat(int columnIndex) throws SQLException
public abstract float getFloat(String columnName) throws SQLException
public abstract int getInt(int columnIndex) throws SQLException
public abstract int getInt(String columnName) throws SQLException
public abstract long getLong(int columnIndex) throws SQLException
public abstract long getLong(String columnName) throws SQLException
public abstract short getShort(int columnIndex) throws SQLException
public abstract short getShort(String columnName) throws SQLException
public abstract String getString(int columnIndex) throws SQLException
public abstract String getString(String columnName) throws SQLException
public abstract Time getTime(int columnIndex) throws SQLException
public abstract Time getTime(String columnName) throws SQLException
public abstract Timestamp getTimestamp(int columnIndex)
        throws SQLException
public abstract Timestamp getTimestamp(String columnName)
        throws SQLException
```

Description

These methods return the specified column value for the current row as the Java data type that matches the method name.

getCursorName()

```
public abstract String getCursorName() throws SQLException
```

Description

Because some databases allow positioned updates, an application needs the cursor name associated with a ResultSet in order to perform those positioned updates. This method provides the cursor name.

getMetaData()

```
public abstract ResultSetMetaData getMetaData() throws SQLException
```

ResultSet *(continued)*

Description

Provides the meta-data object for this `ResultSet`.

getObject()

```
public abstract Object getObject(int columnIndex) throws SQLException
public abstract Object getObject(String columnName) throws SQLException
```

Description

Returns the specified column value for the current row as a Java object. The type returned will be the Java object that most closely matches the SQL type for the column. It is also useful for columns with database-specific data types.

getWarnings()

```
public abstract SQLWarning getWarnings() throws SQLException
```

Description

Returns the first `SQLWarning` object in the warning chain.

next()

```
public abstract boolean next() throws SQLException
```

Description

This method moves the `ResultSet` to the next row. The first call makes the first row the current row. The method returns `true` as long as there is a next row to move to. If there are no further rows to process, it returns `false`. If an `InputStream` from the previous row is still open, it is closed. The `SQLWarning` chain is also cleared.

wasNull()

```
public abstract boolean wasNull() throws SQLException
```

Description

This method returns `true` if the last column read was `null`; otherwise it returns `false`.

ResultSetMetaData

Synopsis

Class Name:	`java.sql.ResultSetMetaData`
Superclass:	None
Immediate Subclasses:	None

ResultSetMetaData (continued)

Interfaces Implemented: None
Availability: New as of JDK 1.1

Description

This class provides meta-information about the types and properties of the columns in a ResultSet instance.

Class Summary

```
public interface ResultSetMetaData {
    static public final int columnNoNulls;
    static public final int columnNullable;
    static public final int columnNullableUnknown;
    // Class Methods
    public abstract String getCatalogName(int column)
        throws SQLException;
    public abstract int getColumnCount() throws SQLException;
    public abstract int getColumnDisplaySize(int column)
        throws SQLException;
    public abstract String getColumnLabel(int column)
        throws SQLException;
    public abstract String getColumnName(int column)
        throws SQLException;
    public abstract int getColumnType(int column) throws SQLException;
    public abstract String getColumnTypeName(int column)
        throws SQLException;
    public abstract int getPrecision(int column) throws SQLException;
    public abstract int getScale(int column) throws SQLException;
    public abstract String getSchemaName(int column)
        throws SQLException;
    public abstract String getTableName(int column)
        throws SQLException;
    public abstract boolean isAutoIncrement(int column)
        throws SQLException;
    public abstract boolean isCaseSensitive(int column)
        throws SQLException;
    public abstract boolean isCurrency(int column) throws SQLException;
    public abstract boolean isDefinitelyWritable(int column)
        throws SQLException;
    public abstract int isNullable(int column) throws SQLException;
    public abstract boolean isReadOnly(int column) throws SQLException;
    public abstract boolean isSearchable(int column)
        throws SQLException;
    public abstract boolean isSigned(int column) throws SQLException;
    public abstract boolean isWritable(int column)
        throws SQLException;
}
```

ResultSetMetaData *(continued)*

Class Methods

getCatalogName()

```
public abstract String getCatalogName(int column) throws SQLException
```

Description

Provides the catalog name associated with the specified column's table.

getColumnCount()

```
public abstract int getColumnCount() throws SQLException
```

Description

Returns the number of columns in the result set.

getColumnDisplaySize()

```
public abstract int getColumnDisplaySize(int column)
      throws SQLException
```

Description

Returns the maximum width for displaying the column's values.

getColumnLabel()

```
public abstract String getColumnLabel(int column) throws SQLException
```

Description

Returns the display name for the column.

getColumnName()

```
public abstract String getColumnName(int column) throws SQLException
```

Description

Returns the database name for the column.

getColumnType()

```
public abstract int getColumnType(int column) throws SQLException
```

Description

Returns the SQL type for the specified column as a value from `java.sql.Types`.

getColumnTypeName()

```
public abstract String getColumnTypeName(int column)
      throws SQLException
```

Description

Returns the name of the SQL type for the specified column.

ResultSetMetaData *(continued)*

getPrecision()

```
public abstract int getPrecision(int column) throws SQLException
```

Description

Returns the number of decimal digits for the specified column.

getScale()

```
public abstract int getScale(int column) throws SQLException
```

Description

Returns the number of digits to the right of the decimal for this column.

getSchemaName()

```
public abstract String getSchemaName(int column) throws SQLException
```

Description

Returns the schema for the table for the specified column.

getTableName()

```
public abstract String getTableName(int column) throws SQLException
```

Description

Returns the name of the table for the specified column.

isAutoIncrement()

```
public abstract boolean isAutoIncrement(int column) throws SQLException
```

Description

Returns true if the column is automatically numbered and therefore read-only.

isCaseSensitive()

```
public abstract boolean isCaseSensitive(int column) throws SQLException
```

Description

Returns true if the column's case is important.

isCurrency()

```
public abstract boolean isCurrency(int column) throws SQLException
```

Description

Returns true if the value for the specified column represents a currency value.

ResultSetMetaData *(continued)*

isDefinitelyWritable()

```
public abstract boolean isDefinitelyWritable(int column)
      throws SQLException
```

Description

Returns `true` if a write operation on the column will definitely succeed.

isNullable()

```
public abstract int isNullable(int column) throws SQLException
```

Description

Returns `true` if `null` values are allowed for the column.

isReadOnly()

```
public abstract boolean isReadOnly(int column) throws SQLException
```

Description

Returns `true` if the column is read-only.

isSearchable()

```
public abstract boolean isSearchable(int column) throws SQLException
```

Description

Returns `true` if the column may be used in a WHERE clause.

isSigned()

```
public abstract boolean isSigned(int column) throws SQLException
```

Description

Returns `true` if the column contains a signed number.

isWritable()

```
public abstract boolean isWritable(int column) throws SQLException
```

Description

Returns `true` if it is possible for a write on a column to succeed.

Statement

Synopsis

Class Name:	`java.sql.Statement`
Superclass:	None

Statement (continued)

Immediate Subclasses:	`java.sql.PreparedStatement`
Interfaces Implemented:	None
Availability:	New as of JDK 1.1

Description

This class represents an embedded SQL statement and is used by an application to perform database access. The closing of a `Statement` automatically closes any open `ResultSet` associated with the `Statement`.

Class Summary

```
public interface Statement {
    // Class Methods
    public abstract void cancel() throws SQLException;
    public abstract void clearWarnings() throws SQLException;
    public abstract void close() throws SQLException;
    public abstract boolean execute(String sql) throws SQLException;
    public abstract ResultSet executeQuery(String sql)
            throws SQLException;
    public abstract int executeUpdate(String sql) throws SQLException;
    public abstract int getMaxFieldSize() throws SQLException;
    public abstract int getMaxRows() throws SQLException;
    public abstract boolean getMoreResults() throws SQLException;
    public abstract int getQueryTimeout() throws SQLException;
    public abstract ResultSet getResultSet() throws SQLException;
    public abstract int getUpdateCount() throws SQLException;
    public abstract SQLWarning getWarnings() throws SQLException;
    public abstract void setCursorName(String name)
            throws SQLException;
    public abstract void setEscapeProcessing(boolean enable)
            throws SQLException;
    public abstract void setMaxFieldSize(int max) throws SQLException;
    public abstract void setMaxRows(int max) throws SQLException;
    public abstract void setQueryTimeout(int seconds)
            throws SQLException;
}
```

Class Methods

`cancel()`

```
public abstract void cancel() throws SQLException
```

Description

In a multi-threaded environment, you can use this method to flag that any processing for this `Statement` in another thread should be

Statement *(continued)*

canceled. In this respect, it is similar to the `stop()` method for `Thread` objects.

clearWarnings() and getWarnings()

```
public abstract void clearWarnings() throws SQLException
public abstract SQLWarning getWarnings() throws SQLException
```

Description

The `clearWarnings()` method allows you to clear all warnings from the warning chain associated with this class. The `getWarnings()` method retrieves the first warning on the chain. You can retrieve any subsequent warnings on the chain using that first warning.

close()

```
public abstract void close() throws SQLException
```

Description

Manually closes the `Statement`. This is generally not required because a `Statement` is automatically closed whenever the `Connection` associated with it is closed.

execute(), executeQuery(), and executeUpdate()

```
public abstract boolean execute(String sql) throws SQLException
public abstract ResultSet executeQuery(String sql) throws SQLException
public abstract int executeUpdate(String sql) throws SQLException
```

Description

Executes the `Statement` by passing the specified SQL to the database. The first method, `execute()`, allows you to execute the `Statement` when you do not know if it is a query or an update. It will return `true` if the statement has result sets to process.

The `executeQuery()` method is used for executing queries. It returns a result set for processing.

The `executeUpdate()` statement is used for executing updates. It returns the number of rows affected by the update.

getMaxFieldSize() and setMaxFieldize()

```
public abstract int getMaxFieldSize() throws SQLException
public abstract void setMaxFieldSize(int max) throws SQLException
```

Description

These methods support the maximum field size attribute that determines the maximum amount of data for any BINARY, VARBINARY, LONGVAR-

Statement *(continued)*

BINARY, CHAR, VARCHAR, and LONGVARCHAR column value. If the limit is exceeded, the excess is silently discarded.

getMaxRows() and setMaxRows()

```
public abstract int getMaxRows() throws SQLException
public abstract void setMaxRows(int max) throws SQLException
```

Description

This attribute represents the maximum number of rows a ResultSet can contain. If this number is exceeded, then any excess rows are silently discarded.

getMoreResults()

```
public abstract boolean getMoreResults() throws SQLException
```

Description

This method moves to the next result and returns true if that result is a ResultSet. Any previously open ResultSet for this Statement is then implicitly closed. If the next result is not a ResultSet or if there are no more results, this method will return false. You can test explicitly for no more results using:

```
(!getMoreResults() && (getUpdateCount() == -1)
```

getQueryTimeout() and setQueryTimeout()

```
public abstract int getQueryTimeout() throws SQLException
public abstract void setQueryTimeout(int seconds) throws SQLException
```

Description

This attribute is the amount of time a driver will wait for a Statement to execute. If the limit is exceeded, an SQLException is thrown.

getResultSet()

```
public abstract ResultSet getResultSet() throws SQLException
```

Description

This method returns the current ResultSet. You should call this only once per result. You never need to call this for executeQuery() calls that return a single result.

getUpdateCount()

```
public abstract int getUpdateCount() throws SQLException
```

Statement (continued)

Description

If the current result was an update, this method returns the number of rows affected by the update. If the result is a ResultSet or if there are no more results, –1 is returned. As with getResultSet(), this method should only be called once per result.

setCursorName()

```
public abstract void setCursorName(String name) throws SQLException
```

Description

This method specifies the cursor name to be used by subsequent State-ment executions. For databases that support positioned updates and deletes, you can then use this cursor name in coordination with any ResultSet objects returned by your execute() or executeQuery() calls to identify the current row for a positioned update or delete. You must use a different Statement object to perform those updates or deletes. This method does nothing for databases that do not support positioned updates or deletes.

setEscapeProcessing()

```
public abstract void setEscapeProcessing(boolean enable)
        throws SQLException
```

Description

Escape processing is on by default. When enabled, the driver will perform escape substitution before sending SQL to the database.

Time

Synopsis

Class Name:	java.sql.Time
Superclass:	java.util.Date
Immediate Subclasses:	None
Interfaces Implemented:	None
Availability:	New as of JDK 1.1

Description

This version of the java.util.Date class maps to an SQL TIME data type.

Time *(continued)*

Class Summary

```
public class Time extends java.util.Date {
    // Class Methods
    static public Time valueOf(String s);
    public Time(int hour, int minute, int second);
    public Time(long time);
    public int getDate();
    public int getDay();
    public int getMonth();
    public int getYear();
    public int setDate(int i);
    public int setMonth(int i);
    public void setTime(long time);
    public void setYear(int i);
    public String toString();
```

Class Methods

getDate(), **setDate()**, **getDay()**, **getMonth()**, **setMonth()**, **getYear()**, and **setYear()**

```
public int getDate()
public int getDay()
public int getMonth()
public int getYear()
public int setDate(int i)
public int setMonth(int i)
public void setYear(int i)
```

Description

These attributes represent the individual segments of a Time object.

setTime()

```
public void setTime(long time)
```

Description

This method sets the Time object to the specified time as the number of seconds since 12:00:00 January 1, 1970 GMT.

Time()

```
public Timestamp(int hour, int minute, intsecond)
public Timestamp(long time)
```

Description

Constructs a new Time object. The first prototype constructs a Time for the hour, minute, and seconds specified. The second constructs one based on the number of seconds since 12:00:00 January 1, 1970 GMT.

Time *(continued)*

toString()

```
public String toString()
```

Description

Formats the Time into a String in the form of hh:mm:ss.

valueOf()

```
static public Timestamp valueOf(String s)
```

Description

Create a new Time based on a String in the form of hh:mm:ss.

Timestamp

Synopsis

Class Name:	java.sql.Timestamp
Superclass:	java.util.Date
Immediate Subclasses:	None
Interfaces Implemented:	None
Availability:	New as of JDK 1.1

Description

This class serves as an SQL representation of the Java Date class specifically designed to serve as an SQL TIMESTAMP. It also provides the ability to hold nanoseconds as required by SQL TIMESTAMP values. You should keep in mind that this class uses the java.util.Date version of hashcode(). This means that two timestamps that differ only by nanoseconds will have identical hash-code() return values.

Class Summary

```
public class Timestamp extends java.util.Date {
    // Class Methods
    static public Timestamp valueOf(String s);
    public Timestamp(int year, int month, int date, int hour,
            int minute, int second, int nano);
    public Timestamp(long time);
    public boolean after(Timestamp t);
    public boolean before(Timestamp t);
    public boolean equals(Timestamp t);
    public int getNanos();
```

Timestamp *(continued)*

```
        public void setNanos(int n);
        public String toString();
}
```

Class Methods

after()

```
public boolean after(Timestamp t)
```

Description

Returns true if this Timestamp is later than the argument.

before()

```
public boolean before(Timestamp t)
```

Description

Returns true if this Timestamp is earlier than the argument.

equals()

```
public boolean equals(Timestamp t)
```

Description

Returns true if the two timestamps are equivalent.

getNanos() and setNanos()

```
public int getNanos()
public void setNanos(int n)
```

Description

This attribute represents the number of nanoseconds for this Timestamp.

Timestamp()

```
public Timestamp(int year, int month, int date, int hour, int minute,
        int second, int nano)
public Timestamp(long time)
```

Description

Constructs a new Timestamp object. The first prototype constructs a Timestamp for the year, month, date, hour, minute, seconds, and nanoseconds specified. The second prototype constructs one based on the number of seconds since 12:00:00 January 1, 1970 GMT.

toString()

```
public String toString()
```

Timestamp *(continued)*

Description

Formats the Timestamp into a String in the form of yyyy-mm-dd hh:mm:ss.fffffffff.

valueOf()

```
static public Timestamp valueOf(String s)
```

Description

Create a new Timestamp based on a String in the form of yyyy-mm-dd hh:mm:ss.fffffffff.

Types

Synopsis

Class Name:	java.sql.Types
Superclass:	java.lang.Object
Immediate Subclasses:	None
Interfaces Implemented:	None
Availability:	New as of JDK 1.1

Description

This class holds static attributes representing SQL data types. These values are the actual constant values defined in the XOPEN specification.

Class Summary

```
public class Types {
    static public final int BIGINT;
    static public final int BINARY;
    static public final int BIT;
    static public final int CHAR;
    static public final int DATE;
    static public final int DECIMAL;
    static public final int DOUBLE;
    static public final int FLOAT;
    static public final int INTEGER;
    static public final int LONGVARBINARY;
    static public final int LONGVARCHAR;
    static public final int NULL;
    static public final int NUMERIC;
    static public final int OTHER;
    static public final int REAL;
```

Types *(continued)*

```
        static public final int SMALLINT;
        static public final int TIME;
        static public final int TIMESTAMP;
        static public final int TINYINT;
        static public final int VARBINARY;
        static public final int VARCHAR;
}
```

Class Methods

This class has no methods.

10

The RMI Classes Used in This Book

This chapter covers a few of the RMI classes we have dealt with in this book. It does not even attempt to cover the full complex set of RMI classes, most of which are never encountered by the RMI developer. Specifically, I have chosen to focus on the classes in this book:

*   `java.rmi.Naming`

*   `java.rmi.Remote`

*   `java.rmi.server.UnicastRemoteObject`

Naming

Synopsis

Class Name:	`java.rmi.Naming`
Superclass:	`java.lang.Object`
Immediate Subclasses:	None
Interfaces Implemented:	None
Availability:	New as of JDK 1.1

Description

This class provides a means for looking up an object based on a URL. The RMI URL is in the form *rmi://host:port/object_name*. You may also use the `Naming` class to bind objects served by the local virtual machine. You may leave out the host and port values in an RMI URL. By default, the host is the local host, and the port is 1099.

214

Naming *(continued)*

Class Summary

```
public final class Naming {
  // Class Methods
  static public void bind(String name, Remote obj)
  throws AlreadyBoundException, MalformedURLException,
        UnknownHostException, RemoteException;

  static public String[] list(String name)
  throws MalformedURLException, UnknownHostException,
        RemoteException;

  static public Remote lookup(String name)
  throws NotBoundException, MalformedURLException,
        UnknownHostException, RemoteException;

  static public void rebind(String name, Remote obj)
  throws MalformedURLException, UnknownHostException, RemoteException;

  static public void unbind(String name)
  throws MalformedURLException, NotBoundException,
        UnknownHostException, RemoteException;
}
```

Class Methods

bind() and rebind()

```
static public void bind(String name, Remote obj)
throws AlreadyBoundException, MalformedURLException,
      UnknownHostException, RemoteException
static public void rebind(String name, Remote obj)
    throws MalformedURLException, UnknownHostException,
          RemoteException
```

Description

These methods allow you to bind an object to a specific URL. They differ only in that rebind() allows you to bind an object to a previously bound URL. On the other hand, bind() will throw an exception if you try to bind an object to a previously bound URL.

list()

```
static public String[] list(String name)
    throws MalformedURLException, UnknownHostException, RemoteException
```

Returns

An array of URLs in the object registry.

Naming *(continued)*

lookup()

```
static public Remote lookup(String name)
    throws NotBoundException, MalformedURLException,
        UnknownHostException, RemoteException
```

Returns

> The remote object bound to the specified URL. In particular, it uses the URL to find the specified remote host and grab a remote object reference for the URL.

unbind()

```
static public void unbind(String name)
    throws MalformedURLException, NotBoundException,
        UnknownHostException, RemoteException
```

Description

> Unbinds the specified URL from any object to which it is bound.

Remote

Synopsis

Class Name: `java.rmi.Remote`
Superclass: None
Immediate Subclasses: None
Interfaces Implemented: None
Availability: New as of JDK 1.1

Description

This interface is extended by all remote interfaces. It prescribes no methods, but instead serves as a way to reference all remote objects.

Class Summary

```
public interface Remote {
}
```

Class Methods

This interface has no methods.

UnicastRemoteObject

Synopsis

Class Name: `java.rmi.UnicastRemoteObject`

Superclass: `java.rmi.server.RemoteServer`

Immediate Subclasses: None

Interfaces Implemented: None

Availability: New as of JDK 1.1

Description

This class is the base class for remote objects. It specifically exports itself upon construction for remote referencing. In addition, it provides the correct semantics for the `hashCode()`, `equals()`, and `toString()` methods. In some cases, it is simply not feasible to extend this class when building a remote object. In those instances, you can get around extending `UnicastRemoteObject` by implementing your own `hashCode()`, `equals()`, and `toString()` methods and calling `UnicastRemoteObject.exportObject()`.

Class Summary

```
public class UnicastRemoteObject extends RemoteServer {
   static public RemoteStub exportObject(Remote obj)
       throws RemoteException;

   public UnicastRemoteObject() throws RemoteException;

   public Object clone() throws CloneNotSupportedException;
}
```

Class Methods

clone()

```
public Object clone() throws CloneNotSupportedException
```

Description

> Returns a clone of the remote object that is distinct from the original.

exportObject()

```
static public RemoteStub exportObject(Remote obj)
       throws RemoteException;
```

Description

> Exports a remote object so that it may be passed across virtual machine boundaries as a remote object

UnicastRemoteObject *(continued)*

UnicastRemoteObject()

> public UnicastRemoteObject() throws RemoteException

Description

> Constructs a new UnicastRemoteObject and calls exportObject()
> on itself.

Index

About the Author

George Reese is an information systems consultant in Bloomington, MN. After earning a degree in philosophy from Bates College in Maine, he worked in television for a while before becoming involved with enterprise client/server and Internet programming. George runs one of the oldest LPMuds on the Internet, Nightmare LPMud, where he developed the Nightmare Object Library used by other muds as a foundation for development. His free textbooks, *LPC_Basics* and *Intermediate LPC*, are widely read by new mud programmers looking to learn LPC. In addition to these works, he has developed a handful of free Internet class libraries for LPC and Java, including the world's first JDBC driver, mSQL-JDBC. When he is not working, he loves skiing, inline skating, and camping. You can find his home page at *http://www.imaginary.com/~borg.*

Colophon

Our look is the result of reader comments, our own experimentation, and feedback from distribution channels. Distinctive covers complement our distinctive approach to technical topics, breathing personality and life into potentially dry subjects.

The image of a jacks game on the cover of *Database Programming with JDBC and Java* is from the CMCD PhotoCD Collection. It was manipulated by Edie Freedman using Adobe Photoshop 3.0 and Adobe Gallery Effects filters. The cover layout was produced with Quark XPress 3.3 using the Bodoni Black font from URW Software.

The inside layout was designed by Nancy Priest. Text was prepared by Mike Sierra in FrameMaker. The heading font is Bodoni BT; the text font is New Baskerville. The illustrations that appear in the book were created in Macromedia Freehand 5.0 by Chris Reilley.

More Titles from O'Reilly

Java Programming

Exploring Java, Second Edition

By Patrick Niemeyer & Joshua Peck
2nd Edition June 1997 (est.)
500 pages (est.), ISBN 1-56592-271-9

The second edition of *Exploring Java*, fully revised to cover Version 1.1 of the JDK, introduces the basics of Java, the object-oriented programming language for networked applications. The ability to create animated World Wide Web pages sparked the rush to Java. But what also makes this language so important is that it's truly portable. The code runs on any machine that provides a Java interpreter, whether Windows 95, Windows NT, the Macintosh, or any flavor of UNIX.

Java in a Nutshell, Second Edition

By David Flanagan
2nd Edition May 1997
650 pages, ISBN 1-56592-262-X

The bestselling Java book just got better. Java programmers migrating to 1.1 find this second edition of Java in a Nutshell contains everything they need to get up to speed.

Newcomers find it still has all of the features that have made it the Java book most often recommended on the Internet. This complete quick reference contains descriptions of all of the classes in the core Java 1.1 API, making it the only quick reference that a Java programmer needs.

Java Virtual Machine

By Troy Downing & Jon Meyer
1st Edition March 1997
440 pages, ISBN 1-56592-194-1

This book is a comprehensive programming guide for the Java Virtual Machine (JVM). It gives readers a strong overview and reference of the JVM so that they may create their own implementations of the JVM or write their own compilers that create Java object code. A Java assembler is provided with the book, so the examples can all be compiled and executed.

Java Language Reference, Second Edition

By Mark Grand
2nd Edition July 1997 (est.)
448 pages, ISBN 1-56592-326-X

The second edition of the *Java Language Reference* is an invaluable tool for Java programmers, especially those who have migrated to Java 1.1. Part of O'Reilly's Java documentation series, this complete reference describes all aspects of the Java language plus new features in Version 1.1, such as inner classes, final local variables and method parameters, anonymous arrays, class literals, and instance initializers.

Java Fundamental Classes Reference

By Mark Grand
1st Edition May 1997
1152 pages , ISBN 1-56592-241-7

The *Java Fundamental Classes Reference* provides complete reference documentation for the Java fundamental classes.

This book takes you beyond what you'd expect from a standard reference manual. Classes and methods are, of course, described in detail. It offers tutorial-style explanations of the important classes in the Java Core API and includes lots of sample code to help you learn by example.

Java AWT Reference

By John Zukowski
1st Edition March 1997
1100 pages, ISBN 1-56592-240-9

With AWT, you can create windows, draw, work with images, and use components like buttons, scrollbars, and pulldown menus. *Java AWT Reference* covers the classes that comprise the java.awt, java.awt.image, and java.applet packages. These classes provide the functionality that allows a Java application to provide user interaction in a graphical environment. It offers a comprehensive explanation of how AWT components fit together with easy-to-use reference material on every AWT class and lots of sample code to help you learn by example.

O'REILLY™

TO ORDER: **800-998-9938** • **order@ora.com** • **http://www.ora.com/**
OUR PRODUCTS ARE AVAILABLE AT A BOOKSTORE OR SOFTWARE STORE NEAR YOU.
FOR INFORMATION: **800-998-9938** • **707-829-0515** • **info@ora.com**

Java Threads

By Scott Oaks and Henry Wong
1st Edition January 1997
252 pages, ISBN 1-56592-216-6

Java Threads is a comprehensive guide to the intricacies of threaded programming in Java, covering everything from the most basic synchronization techniques to advanced topics like writing your own thread scheduler.

Java Threads uncovers the one tricky but essential aspect of Java programming and provides techniques for avoiding deadlock, lock starvation, and other topics.

Java Network Programming

By Elliotte Rusty Harold
1st Edition February 1997
448 pages, ISBN 1-56592-227-1

Java Network Programming is a complete introduction to developing network programs, both applets and applications, using Java; covering everything from networking fundamentals to remote method invocation (RMI).

It also covers what you can do without explicitly writing network code, how you can accomplish your goals using URLs and the basic capabilities of applets.

Developing Java Beans

By Rob Englander
1st Edition June 1997 (est.)
300 pages (est.), ISBN 1-56592-289-1

With *Developing Java Beans,* you'll learn how to create components that can be manipulated by tools like Borland's Latte or Symantec's Visual Cafe, enabling others to build entire applications by using and reusing these building blocks. Beyond the basics, *Developing Java Beans* teaches you how to create Beans that can be saved and restored properly; how to take advantage of introspection to provide more information about a Bean's capabilities; how to provide property editors and customizers that manipulate a Bean in sophisticated ways; and how to integrate Java Beans into ActiveX projects.

Java in a Nutshell, DELUXE EDITION

By various authors
1st Edition June1997 (est.)
ISBN 1-56592-304-9
includes CD-ROM and books.

Java in a Nutshell, Deluxe Edition, is a Java programmer's dream come true in one small package. The heart of this Deluxe Edition is the Java reference library on CD-ROM, which brings together five indispensable volumes for Java developers and programmers, linking related info across books. It includes: *Exploring Java 2nd Edition*, *Java Language Reference, 2nd Edition*, *Java Fundamental Classes Reference*, *Java AWT Reference*, and *Java in a Nutshell, 2nd Edition*, included both on the CD-ROM and in a companion desktop edition. This deluxe library gives you everything you need to do serious programming with Java 1.1.

Database Programming with JDBC and Java

By George Reese
1st Edition July 1997 (est.)
300 pages (est.), ISBN 1-56592-270-0

Java and databases make a powerful combination. Getting the two sides to work together, however, takes some effort— largely because Java deals in objects while most databases do not.

This book describes the standard Java interfaces that make portable,object-oriented access to relational databases possible, and offers a robust model for writing applications that are easy to maintain. It introduces the JDBC and RMI packages and uses them to develop three-tier applications (applications divided into a user interface, an object-oriented logic component, and an information store). Covers Java 1.1.

O'REILLY™

TO ORDER: **800-998-9938** • *order@ora.com* • *http://www.ora.com/*

OUR PRODUCTS ARE AVAILABLE AT A BOOKSTORE OR SOFTWARE STORE NEAR YOU.

FOR INFORMATION: **800-998-9938** • **707-829-0515** • *info@ora.com*

Developing Web Content

World Wide Web Journal

Fourth International World Wide Web Conference Proceedings

A publication of O'Reilly & Associates and the World Wide Web Consortium (W3C)
Winter 1995/96
748 pages, ISBN 1-56592-169-0

The *World Wide Web Journal*, published quarterly, provides timely, in-depth coverage of the W3C's technological developments, such as protocols for security, replication and caching, HTML and SGML, and content labeling. This issue contains 57 refereed technical papers presented at the Fourth International World Wide Web Conference, held December 1995 in Boston, Massachusetts. It also includes the two best papers from regional conferences.

Key Specifications of the World Wide Web

A publication of O'Reilly & Associates and the World Wide Web Consortium (W3C)
Spring 1996
356 pages, ISBN 1-56592-190-9

The key specifications that describe the architecture of the World Wide Web and how it works are maintained online at the World Wide Web Consortium. This issue of the *World Wide Web Journal* collects these key papers in a single volume as an important reference for the Webmaster, application programmer, or technical manager with definitive specifications for the core technologies in the Web.

The Web After Five Years

A publication of O'Reilly & Associates and the World Wide Web Consortium (W3C)
Summer 1996, 226 pp, ISBN 1-56592-210-7

This issue is a reflection on the web after five years. In an interview with Tim Berners-Lee, the inventor of the Web and Director of the W3C, we learn that the Web was built to be an interactive, inter-creative, two-way medium from the beginning. These issues are addressed in selections from the MIT/W3C Workshop on Web Demographics and Internet Survey Methodology, along with commerce-related papers selected from the Fifth International World Wide Web Conference, which took place from May 6–10 in Paris.

Building an Industrial Strength Web

A publication of O'Reilly & Associates and the World Wide Web Consortium (W3C)
Fall 1996, 244 pp, ISBN 1-56592-211-5

Issue 4 focuses on the infrastructure needed to create and maintain an "Industrial Strength Web," from network protocols to application design. Included are the first standard versions of core Web protocols: HTTP/1.1, Digest Authentication, State Management (Cookies), and PICS. This issue also provides guides to the specs, highlighting new features, papers explaining modifications to 1.1 (sticky and compressed headers), extensibility, support for collaborative authoring, and using distributed objects.

Advancing HTML: Style and Substance

A publication of O'Reilly & Associates and the World Wide Web Consortium (W3C)
Winter 1996/97
254 pages, ISBN 1-56592-264-6

This issue is a guide to the specifications and tools that buttress the user interface to the World Wide Web. It includes the latest HTML 3.2 and CSS1 specs, papers on gif animation, JavaScript, Web accessibility, usability engineering, multimedia design, and a report on Amaya.

Scripting Languages: Automating the Web

A publication of O'Reilly & Associates and the World Wide Web Consortium (W3C)
By Lincoln Stein, Clint Wong, Ron Petrusha, Shishir Gundavaram, etc.
Spring 1997, 244 pages, 1-56592-265-4

In spite of all the power built into popular web utilities, the informality, ease, and rapid development cycle of scripting languages make them well suited to the constant change common to most web sites. *Scripting Languages: Automating the Web* guides users and developers in choosing and deploying scripting solutions.

In addition, this issue examines the web-wide impact of Perl as the scripting language of choice for webmasters everywhere, with an in-depth article featuring Perl developers Larry Wall and Tom Christiansen.

C and C++

C++: The Core Language

By Gregory Satir & Doug Brown
1st Edition October 1995
230 pages, ISBN 1-56592-116-X

C++: The Core Language is a first book for
C programmers transitioning to C++, an
object-oriented enhancement of the
C programming language. Designed to
get readers up to speed quickly, this
book thoroughly explains the important con-
cepts and features and gives brief overviews of the rest of the language. Covers features common to all C++ compilers, including
those on UNIX, Windows NT, Windows, DOS, and Macintosh.

Practical C++ Programming

By Steve Oualline
1st Edition September 1995
584 pages, ISBN 1-56592-139-9

Fast becoming the standard language
of commercial software development,
C++ is an update of the C programming
language, adding object-oriented features
that are very helpful for today's larger
graphical applications.

Practical C++ Programming is a complete introduction to the
C++ language for the beginning programmer, and also for C programmers transitioning to C++. Topics covered include good
programming style, C++ syntax (what to use and what not to
use), C++ class design, debugging and optimization, and common programming mistakes. At the end of each chapter are a
number of exercises you can use to make sure you've grasped the
concepts. Solutions to most are provided.

Practical C Programming, Third Edition

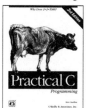

By Steve Oualline
3rd Edition July 1997 (est.)
475 pages(est.), ISBN 1-56592-306-5

There are lots of introductory C books, but
this new edition of Practical C
Programming is the one that has the no-
nonsense, practical approach that has
made Nutshell Handbooks® so popular. C
programming is more than just getting the
syntax right. Style and debugging also play a tremendous part in
creating programs that run well and are easy to maintain.

The third edition of *Practical C Programming* teaches how to
create programs that are easyto read, debug, and maintain. It
features more extensive examples, offers an introduction to
graphical development environments, describes Electronic
Archaeology (the art of going through someone else's code), and
stresses practical rules. The book covers several Windows compilers, in addition to UNIX compilers. Program examples conform
to ANSI C.

Checking C Programs with lint

By Ian F. Darwin
1st Edition October 1988
82 pages, ISBN 0-937175-30-7

The lint program checker has proven time
and again to be one of the best tools for
finding portability problems and certain
types of coding errors in C programs. Lint
verifies a program or program segments
against standard libraries, checks the code
for common portability errors, and tests
the programming against some tried and true guidelines. Linting
your code is a necessary (though not sufficient) step in writing
clean, portable, effective programs. This book introduces you to
lint, guides you through running it on your programs, and helps
you interpret lint's output.

How to stay in touch with O'Reilly

1. Visit Our Award-Winning Web Site

http://www.ora.com/

★ "Top 100 Sites on the Web" —*PC Magazine*
★ "Top 5% Web sites" —*Point Communications*
★ "3-Star site" —*The McKinley Group*

Our web site contains a library of comprehensive product information (including book excerpts and tables of contents), downloadable software, background articles, interviews with technology leaders, links to relevant sites, book cover art, and more. File us in your Bookmarks or Hotlist!

2. Join Our Email Mailing Lists

New Product Releases

To receive automatic email with brief descriptions of all new O'Reilly products as they are released, send email to: **listproc@online.ora.com**
Put the following information in the first line of your message (*not* in the Subject field):
subscribe ora-news "Your Name" of "Your Organization" (for example: subscribe ora-news Kris Webber of Fine Enterprises)

O'Reilly Events

If you'd also like us to send information about trade show events, special promotions, and other O'Reilly events, send email to: **listproc@online.ora.com**
Put the following information in the first line of your message (*not* in the Subject field):
subscribe ora-events "Your Name" of "Your Organization"

3. Get Examples from Our Books via FTP

There are two ways to access an archive of example files from our books:

Regular FTP

- ftp to:
  ftp.ora.com
  (login: anonymous
  password: your email address)
- Point your web browser to:
  ftp://ftp.ora.com/

FTPMAIL

- Send an email message to:
  ftpmail@online.ora.com
  (Write "help" in the message body)

4. Visit Our Gopher Site

- Connect your gopher to:
  gopher.ora.com

- Point your web browser to:
  gopher://gopher.ora.com/

- Telnet to:
  gopher.ora.com
  login: gopher

5. Contact Us via Email

order@ora.com
To place a book or software order online. Good for North American and international customers.

subscriptions@ora.com
To place an order for any of our newsletters or periodicals.

books@ora.com
General questions about any of our books.

software@ora.com
For general questions and product information about our software. Check out O'Reilly Software Online at **http://software.ora.com/** for software and technical support information. Registered O'Reilly software users send your questions to: **website-support@ora.com**

cs@ora.com
For answers to problems regarding your order or our products.

booktech@ora.com
For book content technical questions or corrections.

proposals@ora.com
To submit new book or software proposals to our editors and product managers.

international@ora.com
For information about our international distributors or translation queries. For a list of our distributors outside of North America check out:
http://www.ora.com/www/order/country.html

O'Reilly & Associates, Inc.
101 Morris Street, Sebastopol, CA 95472 USA
TEL   707-829-0515 or 800-998-9938
         (6am to 5pm PST)
FAX   707-829-0104

Titles from O'Reilly

Please note that upcoming titles are displayed in italic.

WEBPROGRAMMING

Apache: The Definitive Guide
Building Your Own Web
  Conferences
Building Your Own Website
CGI Programming for the World
  Wide Web
Designing for the Web
HTML: The Definitive Guide,
  2nd Ed.
JavaScript: The Definitive Guide,
  2nd Ed.
Learning Perl
Programming Perl, 2nd Ed.
Mastering Regular Expressions
WebMaster in a Nutshell
Web Security & Commerce
Web Client Programming with
  Perl
World Wide Web Journal

USING THE INTERNET

Smileys
The Future Does Not Compute
The Whole Internet User's Guide
  & Catalog
The Whole Internet for Win 95
Using Email Effectively
Bandits on the Information
  Superhighway

JAVA SERIES

Exploring Java
Java AWT Reference
Java Fundamental Classes
  Reference
Java in a Nutshell
*Java Language Reference, 2nd
  Edition*
Java Network Programming
Java Threads
Java Virtual Machine

SOFTWARE

WebSite™ 1.1
WebSite Professional™
Building Your Own Web
  Conferences
WebBoard™
PolyForm™
Statisphere™

SONGLINE GUIDES

NetActivism   NetResearch
Net Law   NetSuccess
NetLearning   NetTravel
Net Lessons

SYSTEM ADMINISTRATION

Building Internet Firewalls
Computer Crime: A
  Crimefighter's Handbook
Computer Security Basics
DNS and BIND, 2nd Ed.
Essential System Administration,
  2nd Ed.
Getting Connected: The Internet
  at 56K and Up
Linux Network Administrator's
  Guide
Managing Internet Information
  Services
Managing NFS and NIS
Networking Personal Computers
  with TCP/IP
Practical UNIX & Internet
  Security, 2nd Ed.
PGP: Pretty Good Privacy
sendmail, 2nd Ed.
sendmail Desktop Reference
System Performance Tuning
TCP/IP Network Administration
termcap & terminfo
Using & Managing UUCP
Volume 8: X Window System
  Administrator's Guide
Web Security & Commerce

UNIX

Exploring Expect
Learning VBScript
Learning GNU Emacs, 2nd Ed.
Learning the bash Shell
Learning the Korn Shell
Learning the UNIX Operating
  System
Learning the vi Editor
Linux in a Nutshell
Making TeX Work
Linux Multimedia Guide
Running Linux, 2nd Ed.
SCO UNIX in a Nutshell
sed & awk, 2nd Edition
Tcl/Tk Tools
UNIX in a Nutshell: System V
  Edition
UNIX Power Tools
Using csh & tsch
When You Can't Find Your UNIX
  System Administrator
Writing GNU Emacs Extensions

WEB REVIEW STUDIO SERIES

Gif Animation Studio
Shockwave Studio

WINDOWS

Dictionary of PC Hardware and
  Data Communications Terms
Inside the Windows 95 Registry
Inside the Windows 95 File
  System
Windows Annoyances
*Windows NT File System
  Internals*
Windows NT in a Nutshell

PROGRAMMING

Advanced Oracle PL/SQL
  Programming
Applying RCS and SCCS
C++: The Core Language
Checking C Programs with lint
DCE Security Programming
Distributing Applications Across
  DCE & Windows NT
Encyclopedia of Graphics File
  Formats, 2nd Ed.
Guide to Writing DCE
  Applications
lex & yacc
Managing Projects with make
Mastering Oracle Power Objects
Oracle Design: The Definitive
  Guide
Oracle Performance Tuning, 2nd
  Ed.
Oracle PL/SQL Programming
Porting UNIX Software
POSIX Programmer's Guide
POSIX.4: Programming for the
  Real World
Power Programming with RPC
Practical C Programming
Practical C++ Programming
Programming Python
Programming with curses
Programming with GNU Software
Pthreads Programming
Software Portability with imake,
  2nd Ed.
Understanding DCE
Understanding Japanese
  Information Processing
UNIX Systems Programming for
  SVR4

BERKELEY 4.4 SOFTWARE DISTRIBUTION

4.4BSD System Manager's
  Manual
4.4BSD User's Reference Manual
4.4BSD User's Supplementary
  Documents
4.4BSD Programmer's Reference
  Manual
4.4BSD Programmer's
  Supplementary Documents
X Programming
Vol. 0: X Protocol Reference
  Manual
Vol. 1: Xlib Programming Manual
Vol. 2: Xlib Reference Manual
Vol. 3M: X Window System User's
  Guide, Motif Edition
Vol. 4M: X Toolkit Intrinsics
  Programming Manual, Motif
  Edition
Vol. 5: X Toolkit Intrinsics
  Reference Manual
Vol. 6A: Motif Programming
  Manual
Vol. 6B: Motif Reference Manual
Vol. 6C: Motif Tools
Vol. 8 : X Window System
  Administrator's Guide
Programmer's Supplement for
  Release 6
X User Tools
The X Window System in a
  Nutshell

CAREER & BUSINESS

Building a Successful Software
  Business
The Computer User's Survival
  Guide
Love Your Job!
Electronic Publishing on CD-
  ROM

TRAVEL

Travelers' Tales: Brazil
Travelers' Tales: Food
Travelers' Tales: France
Travelers' Tales: Gutsy Women
Travelers' Tales: India
Travelers' Tales: Mexico
Travelers' Tales: Paris
Travelers' Tales: San Francisco
Travelers' Tales: Spain
Travelers' Tales: Thailand
Travelers' Tales: A Woman's
  World

O'REILLY™

TO ORDER: **800-998-9938** • **order@ora.com** • **http://www.ora.com/**
OUR PRODUCTS ARE AVAILABLE AT A BOOKSTORE OR SOFTWARE STORE NEAR YOU.
FOR INFORMATION: **800-998-9938** • **707-829-0515** • **info@ora.com**

International Distributors

UK, Europe, Middle East and Northern Africa (except France, Germany, Switzerland, & Austria)

INQUIRIES
International Thomson Publishing Europe
Berkshire House
168-173 High Holborn
London WC1V 7AA, United Kingdom
Telephone: 44-171-497-1422
Fax: 44-171-497-1426
Email: itpint@itps.co.uk

ORDERS
International Thomson Publishing Services, Ltd.
Cheriton House, North Way
Andover, Hampshire SP10 5BE,
United Kingdom
Telephone: 44-264-342-832
  (UK orders)
Telephone: 44-264-342-806
  (outside UK)
Fax: 44-264-364418 (UK orders)
Fax: 44-264-342761 (outside UK)
UK & Eire orders: itpuk@itps.co.uk
International orders: itpint@itps.co.uk

France

Editions Eyrolles
61 bd Saint-Germain
75240 Paris Cedex 05
France
Fax: 33-01-44-41-11-44

FRENCH LANGUAGE BOOKS
All countries except Canada
Phone: 33-01-44-41-46-16
Email: geodif@eyrolles.com

ENGLISH LANGUAGE BOOKS
Phone: 33-01-44-41-11-87
Email: distribution@eyrolles.com

Australia

WoodsLane Pty. Ltd.
7/5 Vuko Place, Warriewood NSW 2102
P.O. Box 935, Mona Vale NSW 2103
Australia
Telephone: 61-2-9970-5111
Fax: 61-2-9970-5002
Email: info@woodslane.com.au

Germany, Switzerland, and Austria

INQUIRIES
O'Reilly Verlag
Balthasarstr. 81
D-50670 Köln
Germany
Telephone: 49-221-97-31-60-0
Fax: 49-221-97-31-60-8
Email: anfragen@oreilly.de

ORDERS
International Thomson Publishing
Königswinterer Straße 418
53227 Bonn, Germany
Telephone: 49-228-97024 0
Fax: 49-228-441342
Email: order@oreilly.de

Asia (except Japan & India)

INQUIRIES
International Thomson Publishing Asia
60 Albert Street #15-01
Albert Complex
Singapore 189969
Telephone: 65-336-6411
Fax: 65-336-7411

ORDERS
Telephone: 65-336-6411
Fax: 65-334-1617
thomson@signet.com.sg

New Zealand

WoodsLane New Zealand Ltd.
21 Cooks Street (P.O. Box 575)
Wanganui, New Zealand
Telephone: 64-6-347-6543
Fax: 64-6-345-4840
Email: info@woodslane.com.au

Japan

O'Reilly Japan, Inc.
Kiyoshige Building 2F
12-Banchi, Sanei-cho
Shinjuku-ku
Tokyo 160 Japan
Telephone: 81-3-3356-5227
Fax: 81-3-3356-5261
Email: kenji@ora.com

India

Computer Bookshop (India) PVT. LTD.
190 Dr. D.N. Road, Fort
Bombay 400 001
India
Telephone: 91-22-207-0989
Fax: 91-22-262-3551
Email: cbsbom@giasbm01.vsnl.net.in

The Americas

O'Reilly & Associates, Inc.
101 Morris Street
Sebastopol, CA 95472 U.S.A.
Telephone: 707-829-0515
Telephone: 800-998-9938 (U.S. &
Canada)
Fax: 707-829-0104
Email: order@ora.com

Southern Africa

International Thomson Publishing
Southern Africa
Building 18, Constantia Park
138 Sixteenth Road
P.O. Box 2459
Halfway House, 1685 South Africa
Telephone: 27-11-805-4819
Fax: 27-11-805-3648

O'REILLY™

O'Reilly & Associates, Inc.
101 Morris Street
Sebastopol, CA 95472-9902
1-800-998-9938

Visit us online at:
http://www.ora.com/
orders@ora.com

O'REILLY WOULD LIKE TO HEAR FROM YOU

Which book did this card come from?

_____

Where did you buy this book?
- ❏ Bookstore
- ❏ Direct from O'Reilly
- ❏ Bundled with hardware/software
- ❏ Other _____

- ❏ Computer Store
- ❏ Class/seminar

What operating system do you use?
- ❏ UNIX
- ❏ Windows NT
- ❏ Other _____

- ❏ Macintosh
- ❏ PC(Windows/DOS)

What is your job description?
- ❏ System Administrator
- ❏ Network Administrator
- ❏ Web Developer
- ❏ Other _____

- ❏ Programmer
- ❏ Educator/Teacher

- ❏ Please send me O'Reilly's catalog, containing a complete listing of O'Reilly books and software.

Name _____   Company/Organization _____

Address _____

City _____   State _____   Zip/Postal Code _____   Country _____

Telephone _____   Internet or other email address (specify network) _____

Nineteenth century wood engraving
of a bear from the O'Reilly &
Associates Nutshell Handbook®
Using & Managing UUCP.

POST CARD

BUSINESS REPLY MAIL
FIRST CLASS MAIL   PERMIT NO. 80   SEBASTOPOL, CA

Postage will be paid by addressee

O'Reilly & Associates, Inc.
101 Morris Street
Sebastopol, CA 95472-9902